KENTUCKY'S EVERYDAY HEROES #2

Kentucky's Everyday Heroes
Volume 2

by Steve Flairty

Foreword by Bill Goodman
Edited by Michael Embry

WIND PUBLICATIONS

International Standard Book Number 978-1-936138-16-6
Library of Congress Control Number 2010927963

First edition

Front cover adapted from a design by Bryant Wells.

To George Schnorr, who lived his faith.

Contents

Acknowledgements

The challenge involved with thanking people publicly for their help in this two-year work is that I may neglect some pretty deserving individuals. I will risk a try because this book surely is a product of many hands.

Mike Embry, my editor, both encourages hope and keeps me humble. He knows what he's doing. I don't know if he was put on earth strictly to help me, but if not just me, I'm one of his primary subjects.

Much gratitude to friends Eric Fruge and Debbie Kohl Kremer—both better writers than me, but who care for my mission and have often plugged my books.

Bill Goodman, who wrote the foreword and has encouraged the work from the beginning, interviews Kentucky heroes regularly on Kentucky Educational Television. We both feel the passion. He has great credibility in the commonwealth, and I thank him profusely.

To my friends I see mornings at Panera Bread, you mean a lot. The fact we seldom agree on politics doesn't matter.

Thanks to those who have invited me to speak at their gatherings, like Grace Gorrell, Peggy Cains, local retired teachers' groups, service clubs and churches around the area. Gratitude, also, should be expressed to the hundreds of school children in Jessamine and Fayette County who have listened intently to *Heroes* stories, as well as their supportive teachers.

Appreciation is in order to the individuals offering hero nominations. Though I didn't use every suggestion made, it's comforting to know that there is such a nice pool from which to draw. I'll continue to need your ideas in the future.

Special thanks also to the following employees at the Goodwill Stores, where I look for reading material at bargain prices: Victor,

Denny, Molli, Darlene, Sandy, Fawn, Steve, Patia, Candace, Christiana and Terry. You always ask, "How's the book coming? when you should ask, "Why aren't you home writing?"

Thanks so much to the following for a variety of reasons: Rick Landon, Dave English, Laura Ebert, Gin Perry, Eugene and Alma Flairty, Roger Singleton, Suzanne Isaacs, Morgan Alexander, Tracy Gatliff, and Shannon Greene (who long ago typed my manuscripts when I first got the hankering to write for publication).

And to those featured in the profiles, the heroes themselves: Without you, there's no book at all.

Foreword

Years ago, when I was in grade school in Glasgow, Kentucky, I used to scamper down College Street after the bell rang and head for the Mary Wood Weldon Library. It was a magical place filled with adventure and surprises and, if a ten-year-old Little Leaguer would admit to it—a bit of knowledge, too.

Running up the steps between the stone columns that flanked the heavy glass front door, I'd be welcomed by the musty smell of hundreds of books and magazines. I remember distinctly my reading spot: tucked between the two long, smooth, dark wooden bookshelves with just enough room for a scrawny kid in short pants to crumple to the floor and reach for an afternoon's delight. My reading pleasure for the moment came in blue, hardcover book binding. Along the spine the subject of the biography was spelled out clearly: Abraham Lincoln, George Washington, Daniel Boone, and Helen Keller. I devoured them and vowed to read everyone in the series before the first pitch of the summer league was thrown in just a few weeks. These little blue books were history, travel, exploration and exhilaration, and over the years they've served their purpose well.

In Steve Flairty's first volume of *Kentucky's Everyday Heroes: Ordinary People Doing Extraordinary Things*, we learned about an array of exceptional Kentuckians, who in their own right might be as exemplary as Lincoln or Boone. In fact, I would consider them our modern-day Boones. Remarkable citizens of the Commonwealth like Prestonburg's John Rosenberg, who has labored long in eastern Kentucky for the Appalachian Research and Defense Fund (Appalred); Father John Rauch, a Glenmary priest, who's been fighting for truth and justice in the hills of Appalachia for over thirty years; and Dr. John Belanger, a physician living in Berea, who gave up a pretty good medical practice just so he could open up an affordable medical clinic in Paint Lick. If you missed those stories, (you really need to include the first edition in your library), I'm sure Steve would be glad to send you a copy.

Steve called these subjects his "family of heroes." He told me long before the publication of the first edition that he would be gathering more stories for a second volume. He'd discovered a wealth of wonderful, warm, accomplished folks that deserved their own place among the hall of heroes he had created. He not only mined a variety of contacts, associates, friends and his family of heroes for more material…he asked the readers of *Kentucky's Everyday Heroes* to send in their inspirational submissions. Flairty's mailbox and e-mail account must have been stuffed with interesting and colorful characters because he has put together another outstanding selection of Kentuckians to include in this edition.

Steve writes about "The Can Man," Charles Whitaker of River, Kentucky, who collects and recycles aluminum cans and then donates the proceeds to a school in Johnson County; Dale Faughn, an eighty-four-year-old who is in his sixtieth year of teaching at Caldwell County High School; Evelyn Johnson Seals, a lady in Middlesboro who operates "The Blessing House," a room in her house dedicated to giving needed items to the poor; and Robin Schmidt, a Delta Airlines flight attendant from Covington who sends monthly "care" packages to U.S. military personnel overseas.

On more than one occasion, I've been known to "borrow" a few of these fascinating folks as subjects for my "One to One" conversation program on Kentucky Educational Television. Also, I'll confess that in order to indulge my guilty pleasure and interest in all things Kentucky, I've arranged to coerce my wife and some of our friends for a trek to East and West Kentucky to meet up with some of Flairty's subjects.

I can't wait to meet Bill Gordon. Steve writes that Gordon, who operates the High Adventure Wilderness School from 500 rugged, hilly, pristine acres of mostly wooded area near Menifee County, just east of Stanton, in Powell County went "green" long before it became trendy. Sounds like a road trip to me!

Dr. George Wright is another person you should know. Wright grew up poor and disadvantaged in Lexington's Charlotte Court housing project over fifty years ago. But because his mother taught him there were "no excuses for not doing well in school," today Wright is a renowned historian and president of Prairie View A&M University in Texas.

Steve Flairty has done it again!

Whether in a small town library or big city bookstore or huddled comfortably in my favorite reading chair, the second edition of *Kentucky's Everyday Heroes* will be my guide and introduction to a whole new assortment of friends. Friends that I will want to know more about and want to visit, true Kentuckians who make up the rich fabric of a beautiful and alluring state that we should celebrate every day.

I hope they are part of your next Kentucky adventure, too.

— BILL GOODMAN
Producer/host of "Kentucky Tonight,"
"One to One" and "Bookclub@ket"
on Kentucky Educational Television

Introduction

There are few places I'd rather be than standing in front of a group of engaged persons and sharing a sampling of stories from *Kentucky's Everyday Heroes*. I've enjoyed that opportunity over forty times in the last two years. It's at these times that I sense a real connection to the listeners, not because of my eloquence, but because of the stories I'm blessed to relate about Kentuckians who live heroically each day.

Allow me to bring to sharper focus who I mean by Kentucky's everyday heroes. Seldom do I talk about the well-known people whom we see on TV, the movies or radio, though there are among them individuals who both entertain and act courageously, or even greatly sacrifice for others. A case in point would be Tim Farmer, whose biography I published in 2005. Tim overcame the loss of the use of his right arm to become the dynamic host of an outdoors TV show on public television. He's also one who spends time teaching and encouraging others who have had lost limbs or experienced other debilitating conditions.

Neither do I report to my audiences accounts of sports stars who get big hits or make pressure-packed field goals, though they can be considered admirable for performing at such high skill levels. These athletes are entertaining and lend a bit of excitement to our lives, but heroic acts more often take place off the court or field.

Too, it's not uncommon to hear of individuals, who in a moment of need, are daring and risk their lives to rescue other humans' lives. So thankful for their presence of mind to act quickly, decisively and to put someone's life before theirs. But even they are not the ones I offer tribute here.

The special spirits I wish to highlight are often, simply, over-comers. They're the ones who haven't let physical disabilities, or brutally tough childhoods, or life's failures get them down. You get the idea. They may get knocked down but they get up from the ground, shake themselves off, and work through the challenges facing them. They do it consistently, and over time. They not only survive, but thrive and show us all what is possible against great odds.

Many are givers. Not necessarily of money and things, but givers of time, effort—and sometimes of their dreams—to unselfishly improve others' lives. These Kentuckians often are known only by those in their communities, though some get a wider following as their stories unfold. Two in this book, for example, were subjects of national media stories.

My everyday heroes, representing Kentucky, go out and present their noble lives daily, a gift to us all. People watch them, learn from them, and are inspired by them. Almost unwittingly, they can move their observers to higher acts of character.

But these true heroes don't see that they're anything special. They wonder why people make such a fuss about them.

With the words that are written here, I hope that the reader will see why so many do see my everyday heroes as special, and that there's a good reason to make such a fuss about them.

Kentucky's Everyday Heroes #2 follows the first *Heroes* book with twenty-three more profiles of inspiration mined from areas all around the state. You'll meet people like humble and reserved Charles Whitaker, nicknamed "The Can Man," who recycles aluminum cans to raise money for a Christian school.

In Lexington, a plastic surgeon has brought a host of his medical peers, plus many others, together on one Sunday morning a month to give working people who can't afford health insurance access to important medical surgical care. No fees are charged, and the medical personnel give of their time and skills free.

A public middle-school teacher from western Kentucky sponsored a Junior Optimist club that became the largest in the world, and in so doing, touched in positive ways thousands of vulnerable citizens, both in his community and internationally.

Going far beyond her expected duties, a flight attendant from Covington has become a passionate advocate for America's military servicemen, engaging her passengers meaningfully in the endeavor. It all starts with her asking that they contribute some words of encouragement in a journal she passes down the aisles.

And in Madison County, a quiet-spoken Boy Scout seeking designation as an Eagle Scout chose a project that would give lasting tribute to those from his county who died in Lexington's Bluegrass Airport's tragic Flight 5191 airline crash in August, 2006. He helped raise $27,000 to fund a beautiful memorial to the six victims. Pretty mature stuff for a sixteen-year-old, indeed, and a hero among peers and of all age ranges.

In the twenty-three profiles, a total of twenty-seven featured heroes are included. Interspersed are other admirable individuals who play their supportive parts, those who helped my subjects become the best they could be. Though not featured, they're doubtlessly significant. Iron sharpens iron, it is said.

Truly, Kentucky is like all areas of the United States in that the state has its own set of problems that beg to be addressed. No one can disagree that we have economic challenges, health concerns, drug abuse issues and over-populated prisons, to name a few. But we also have the benefit of quality human resources, namely a bountiful share of some of the most caring, most unselfish, most committed and brave persons anywhere.

I'm blessed, and proud, to help shine light on a few of the special individuals who live in a special state. Doing that has become an important part of who I am.

I hope this selection of profiles adds a lasting, positive bent to the fabric of your life, too.

The Heroes

Charles Whitaker

"The Can Man" Quietly Helps School Children

Though the sign on the back of his pickup truck says "Free road maps to heaven," he is a quiet, reserved man.

He's not unfriendly, just a bit shy; his soft and forgiving eyes give signal that he is gentle and comes in peace. Truly, he is a good, giving and *forgiving* man. That's obvious, but because of the way he chooses to carry out his ministry to children, the folks around these parts call him "The Can Man."

Charles Whitaker, ninety-years-old, still gets around well for one so advanced in his time on earth. So well that most days, excluding Sunday when he goes to church, the white-haired and slightly built Whitaker can be seen around the Paintsville community, mostly around parking lots.

There, he patiently and meticulously collects aluminum soft drink cans to sell at a recycling center in Prestonsburg. He might also be found with his Ford Ranger at a neighbor's house, answering the call that "they had some cans to give me." On Saturdays, he is at the Paintsville stockyards, where, he says, "I pick up cans all day, even in the winter, four or five bags..."

Whitaker could also be down in Cort Daniel's basement in his tiny recycle-processing plant—headquarters, one might say—for his environmentally friendly and noble project.

Whitaker gets paid about seventy-five cents per pound for his trouble, then promptly hands the funds over to the local Johnson County Christian School, in Paintsville—with no strings attached.

"I just take the money and receipts right over to the school and give to 'em," he said in his drawl. He doesn't bother to reimburse his gasoline money from the proceeds.

Charles Whitaker, assisted by great, great niece Rachel Hitchcock

Whitaker's been collecting cans for this purpose for about sixteen years, and he can tell you nearly to the dime how much money he has raised (nearing $36,000), and he can also tell you how many cans he has collected and turned in. "Two million, working on three million. It just adds up," he said. He also is on the use of his third pick-up truck since he started his project; one wore out, the second wrecked.

Johnson County Christian School has about sixty-seven students and serves the kindergarten to eighth grade population. Jim McKenzie, who formerly sat on the board of directors, said the money that Whitaker raises is "often used to help the families of kids who are behind in their payments to the school. It's so good to see people get involved in something like this for no personal reasons other than they just want to help. He does it sometimes when he's not feeling well. I've seen him working when he was so weak he should have been in bed."

Whitaker spent twenty-three years in the U.S. Air Force and followed that with a fourteen-year stint as a manager of a liquor store in Ohio, but he left after a Christian-religious conversion. He now resides with his lifelong friend, Cort Daniel, and Cort's wife Ruby, in the tiny town of River, about seven miles from Paintsville.

Whitaker has not been without a little adventure, the unwanted kind, in carrying out his project. There was the surly-mannered individual, who, seeing Whitaker crushing cans in a store parking lot, verbally attacked him. "The man told me that people were saying I was nothing but the belly of a snake who would stoop to do what I was doing," Whitaker said. "But I forgave him and I don't have any hard feelings."

A few years ago, while he and his friend Cort were hauling cans in Whitaker's Ranger, a driver collided into the side of their vehicle, and Whitaker was seriously hurt. Whitaker said, "I spent nineteen days in the hospital. I had to go out and get another Ranger to drive, but I don't have anything against that man, either."

5

Besides the helping hand he often gets from Cort Daniel, does anybody else work with Whitaker?

"Sometimes people ask to help, but they want to know how much money they'll make," said Whitaker, who also flattens his cans with a sledgehammer.

Kelly Caudill is involved with Johnson County Christian School, and he's known Whitaker for nearly twenty years. "Charles is a man of few words," said Caudill, "but he has made a difference in the Christian school here. I also know he helps with six or seven other ministries, too."

Whitaker is not one to brag, though. "He's humble, and he's always been that way," said Kym Hitchcock, Whitaker's great niece.

Whitaker doesn't fashion himself as an Al Gore environmentalist or any kind of hero. He just fell into his project somewhat by happenstance. "There was a lady about ninety-years-old who asked me to start doing the cans for the school," Whitaker said. "She had to quit. It was something to do. I didn't have anything else to do so I got started doing it. What I do, I do to help the kids."

Looking at how the whole noble and successful operation developed over the years, what would Whitaker do different about his recycling project? After some thought, he said, "I'd probably do some advertising to get my cans faster."

By now, most in the community know that "The Can Man" is looking for their cans. They are appreciative and respectful for what he does. So, too, are all the people who are involved with the Johnson County Christian School.

Kevin Gunderson

Policeman Survives Shooting
to Make His Mark in City Government

It was a scorching Friday afternoon, July 18, 1980, when Officer Kevin Gunderson of the Ashland Police Department was practicing his rounds at the shooting range.

Gunderson, on duty at another location because he was subbing for a buddy who asked for a day off, relished the action and excitement that his badge promised him—almost as much as his passion for golf. So with youthful exuberance and confidence, the twenty-four-year-old responded quickly when a call came to assist the Boyd County Sheriff's Department in serving a tricky non-support warrant case.

The buzz was that the matter at hand could potentially be dangerous, and Gunderson would find that it was. With two deputies accompanying him, one with Gunderson entering a dilapidated house and the other standing watch outside, the situation got nasty real fast.

Gunderson remembers clearly the ugliness when the person in violation was confronted bedside with his girlfriend. "The man asked to see the warrant," he said, "and when I did show it, he pulled a gun from under the pillow and shot me in the neck. I shot him at the same time, and I fell down instantly, paralyzed."

Kevin Gunderson

The assailant was shot two more times by the deputy—but, ironically, was able to walk handcuffed to the police car. Some things don't seem fair, as Gunderson has not taken a step since, and is confined to navigating himself in a well-used wheelchair. He characterizes the changing of a life in an instant this way: "I went from six-feet-four to four-feet-six. I didn't think I would be around very long."

But he has been around a long time, and though it's been a painful struggle at times, Gunderson has more than survived. He's thrived, and in doing so has helped better the lives of thousands in his community. Just ask the folks around Ashland, where he has served nine terms as a city commissioner, from 1990 to the present, including a stint as acting mayor in the summer of 2008 when Mayor Steve Gilmore resigned to become Boyd County school superintendent.

Gunderson often receives the most votes for the commission race and has been instrumental in such successful issues as the Town Center Mall and the Riverfront development, sewer-line upgrading, and helping foster a sense of pride in Ashland, as in the renovated Paramount Arts Center. Through sending on-line "Kevin Mail," keeping an informative web site, and being out and available in public, communication with constituents is fostered. He both inspires others by being an overcomer and, simply, by getting things done for welfare of the local citizens.

Raymond Graeves, former president and CEO of the Ashland Chamber of Commerce, praised the dynamic Gunderson. "I believe he is the most effective and, arguably, diligent member of the commission. He is always prepared and seems to be at every community activity."

The yearly salary for Gunderson's commission work is only $6,500, but the people in the Boyd County area have appreciated Gunderson's service so much that they have helped finance two modified vans, allowing him to make his driving rounds by himself. "I owe them and the police department so much. They have always supported me through everything," he said.

Looking back, two policeman colleagues in particular are praised by Gunderson for their undying support in the aftermath of the 1980 shooting—Chief Ron McBride and recently retired chief Tom Kelley. They remain close today. McBride helped pave the way for Gunderson's transport to a Chicago hospital, termed "his best opportunity for recovery" by McBride. From Chicago, the aggressive demeanor of McBride helped facilitate a move to a

Canadian hospital for neural surgery. Kelley, according to McBride, "was involved with the emotional side and dealt with Kevin the person. Tom was the friend, the advocate…the bearer of bad news."

Amazingly, nine months after the shooting and following an intense period of rehabilitation, Gunderson was again working for the Ashland Police Department by April of 1981—this time as a dispatcher and part of a new emergency communications system.

"I handled the first 911 call in Ashland," he said. The logistics of the matter, which involved adapting the equipment to Gunderson's special physical needs, were daunting. According to McBride, Gunderson's attitude was "We're going to make this work."

And it did work. Buoyed by the creative workmanship of mechanical problem solvers McBride had recruited, the wounded policeman handled his position with graceful aplomb through 1988, then began to feel the gentle tug of politics.

"I had always been interested in politics and had been helping others run for office, so I decided to give it a try for myself," said Gunderson, who won his first race in 1989, took office in 1990 and remains there today. He plans to continue working in Ashland—though he has had others suggest a try at the Kentucky General Assembly. On moving his work to the state level, Gunderson was pointed: "Here, I'm one of five. In Frankfort, I'd be one of 100. I believe I can be more effective in Ashland, so I'll probably stay."

Gunderson carries out his daily government duties with vigor—after first spending ninety minutes every morning, because of physical challenges, "just getting ready to start my day," he said with a grin. "And then the gas company sends me a Christmas card every year because I just love taking long showers and keep the house warm. But I have now actually spent more time in my life as a wheelchair user than ambulatory."

Most of his daily aggravations he handles with learned patience, but understandably bristles at those who would wrongfully use handicapped-parking spaces. "There are too many people who have the parking passes who shouldn't be using them and it blocks the places for people who need them," Gunderson said.

There was the accident in 1999 when Gunderson fell while getting off an airplane, the result being that "I'm a little more paralyzed than I was in 1998."

Before that problem, however, he fought through the legal system for denied workers compensation payments, a case that ultimately was decided in 1986 in the Kentucky Supreme Court—in Gunderson's favor. "That was the most stressful thing that has happened to me," he said.

McBride is not surprised by his friend and colleague's courageous and proactive way of doing things. "Kevin was a hero before he was injured," said McBride. "He had a passion for highway safety, and when he was twenty-two or twenty-three he started a program for high school students in the county. I believe that if he'd not been injured that his future might have been working for the governor in highway safety."

Gunderson admitted that it took the high school presentations to help him get over the fear of speaking in front of groups. "I really enjoyed speaking after doing that," he said. Along with opportunities in the Ashland area, he still manages time to appear in front of school classes today.

But to the community of Ashland, Kevin Gunderson's inspirational life of courage and service rings clearly every day.

Robin Schmidt

'Flying the Friendly Skies' with Compassion

Robin Schmidt can't wait to board her next commercial airline flight—and the next, and the next. The blond-haired and perky forty-eight-year-old woman from Covington absolutely revels in traveling to interesting, faraway places, but that's not the only reason she enjoys flying.

Schmidt, as a Delta flight attendant, sees each oncoming group of passengers she greets with enthusiastic eyes, as partners in a grand mission. She wants her passenger friends to join her in a project of caring, one she says "makes my job more intrinsically rewarding."

Just take a typical day on the job, starting with a friendly smile as passengers board the airliner. Schmidt gives the usual welcoming greeting and appropriate safety information, then she adds an extra little announcement—a challenge. She tells of her passion for recognizing the service of U.S. troops, explaining how they often feel lonely and disengaged, and how there is a way to help.

"I'll pass around a journal," she says to the Delta travelers, "and I'll give you an opportunity to write some upbeat words, tell a joke or maybe even a prayer…anything you would want to read if you were far away from home. This will give encouragement to the serviceman I'm currently supporting."

Robin Schmidt

No one is forced to participate, she emphasizes to all. Then Schmidt continues by telling the now fully engaged listeners of the "care" packages she sends monthly and that anyone interested in providing help would be greatly appreciated.

Since Schmidt started making her appeal five years ago the response has been amazingly good, almost overwhelming at times.

"I have never had a negative word written in any of the journals," she said, "and you wouldn't believe all the nice people who give me a dollar, a five or more to use for our troops."

Then there is the wonderful couple who started out by giving Schmidt $100 each for three servicemen, but their giving didn't end there.

"Every three or four months, they send a check for $500," said Schmidt. "Last summer, the gentleman sent me a check and said to me, 'I know you'll do the right thing with it.'"

She was shocked when she saw the couple had donated $5,000.

"I was in communication with one of my soldiers serving in Iraq who had talked about buying a truck when he came back from deployment," Schmidt said. "He told me his price range, and the $5,000 check more than covered it. But even when someone gives me just one dollar, I am so blessed."

In the last year, Schmidt has found donors who financed $2,100 toward her informal "Mail Call for Heroes" drive. The money is used for buying phone cards for the troops, "one of the favorite things they want," said Schmidt.

She's communicated with eighty-four troops since January 2002, and her care packages have been explosions of joy as they arrive in war-torn Iraq or Afghanistan, often between two to six weeks after shipping. Besides the all-important journals that are packed, the other items in the packages are thoughtfully conceived and include toiletries, snacks, and gag gifts like "silly string" and stuffed Tigger animal piñatas.

Piñatas?

"It's very important that troops can build trust with the locals," said Schmidt. "They might tell our troops where an improvised explosive device is buried, for example. This saves lives. The kids really like breaking open the piñatas, which they had never heard about before."

The stuffed Tiggers are a big hit, and Schmidt receives a lot of feedback in the form of pictures. "That's all I really want in return," she said, "just send me a lot of pictures of their response when they receive the packages, or a quick note, so I know if they like what I sent."

Sgt. Timothy Gallagher is stationed in Afghanistan and is an appreciative recipient of Schmidt's caring gestures. "Robin has been such a blessing to me and all the soldiers she supports," said Gallagher. "Not only does she do good and kind things for me, she also does them for my unit and the locals. Much of the things she sends are shared with the local school children. She really goes above and beyond the call of duty when sending extremely thoughtful gifts and also everyday items that are needed and hard to get a hold of here in theater."

Schmidt received similar praise from former National Guard serviceman, Sgt. Ed Rees. "It is an easy thing to say the words, 'I support the troops,' but in my experience it is a rare individual who actually follows through with action on those words," remarked Rees.

Schmidt has engaged students at the local Taylor Mill Elementary School, near Covington, in writing cards and letters to soldiers overseas who are being treated at hospitals. Principal Lois White called it "a fabulous program, with the whole school involved."

White has started corresponding with a nineteen-year-old troop due to Schmidt's influence. "We don't want our troops to ever be forgotten," said White, "and our school kids write the letters three or four times a year."

Schmidt spends at least twenty hours a week with her military project, much of the time in a post office, but she has also carved out time to visit and support an orphanage in South Africa where a loving married couple has rescued orphaned children off the streets and provided physical, spiritual, and emotional support.

"Sharon and Grant are two amazing people," said Schmidt. "I have gone to the orphanage, near Johannesburg, as part of the Airline Ambassadors program, and have gone numerous times on my own. I think of the children there as part of my family."

For Schmidt, her life growing up in Seattle was, at the least, challenging. She was molested as a child, and she spent many years in counseling, a process "which helped me a lot," she said. "I don't mind that being out in public because it has made me what I am today."

She also had difficulty relating to both parents, though later as an adult she developed a close relationship with her father. "They both died about fifteen years ago, and I had a very difficult time with it," she said.

As she struggled through her tough teenage years, Schmidt developed a deep Christian faith that, she says, "I would be nothing without."

She sees her on-going project to support the troops, along with her compassion toward vulnerable children in South Africa, as simply carrying out her part in "God working through me. I don't think I'm anything special. I'm just an instrument."

Though Schmidt is an affable spirit, one not easily bothered by testy, difficult people, she gets very disappointed at those who accuse her of being "political" in giving and garnering support for the U.S. military troops.

She makes it clear that she has no interest in the politics of the issue. "It's all about individual sacrifices I'm trying to honor, and I know other people are getting involved because of what I'm doing," she said.

Delta flight attendant colleague Joanna Morton calls Schmidt "the most unselfish, caring, honest person I know."

Morton observed that Schmidt was in New York when the 9–11 terrorist attack occurred. "That event affected her so much, and her project is her calling—her passion," said Morton, whose church in Ohio recently gave a significant financial gift to Schmidt's work.

Because of Schmidt's travels, her projects and her natural extroverted nature, she's acquired a network of admirers and extended family all around the U.S., and even internationally. Her words uplift and exude gratitude.

A few entries she wrote to friends in Facebook recently demonstrate her positive persona:

"Thanks so much for your support."

"It's not about me, it's about our troops."

"Am thankful to have been able to support your brother."

"My day is packed with shopping for monthly care packages."

"There is no greater joy than making a difference for others."

Recently, a newspaper article in the *Cincinnati Enquirer* profiling Schmidt sent her unique story rocketing all over the nation. Soon after the story was published in Cincinnati, Schmidt made appearances on Fox News, ABC News as "Person of the Week," and was profiled in *People* magazine. During a two-hour period after her story went national, Schmidt received 500 e-mails showing support and asking about ways to help.

She has also found new ways to support the troops, one of which is visiting and serving at the USO Wounded Warrior Center in Germany. The exposure has taken Schmidt's work to another level, but she has no plans for a more formal organization to develop.

"I want to keep it very personal," she said. "Big organizations sometimes lose the personal touch."

Schmidt's love and appreciation for all who risk their lives in military service is, in fact, very personal. She thinks about them in the morning when she awakens, when she lays down at night. She thinks of them while she tends to the needs of Delta flight passengers flying all over the world. She thinks about adding that extra bit of care to the care packages—a special kind of snack food, something representing the favorite team of a recipient, the piñatas, the "silly string."

But always, there are the journals…

Said Ed Rees: "The care packages she puts together are unbelievable. But, without a doubt, the best thing Robin has done is to allow others to share in her endeavor and connect with servicemen through her journals. Reading through the journals I received, something I still do, connects me with Americans in a way I didn't know was possible."

She prefers to put the focus back on soldiers like Gallagher and Rees. "I am here for our valiant heroes who put themselves on the line, every single day. Our military members sacrifice more than anyone of us can imagine in a day," Schmidt said.

It seems fitting that Schmidt makes her living by working—and serving—way up high in the clouds. If you think about it, it simply puts her that much closer to her ultimate destination, where she will win her own special pair of wings, and where others will journal kind thoughts toward her legacy.

But in the here and now, Schmidt repeatedly makes it plain what motivates her work: "I never want any of our troops to ever feel alone on the battlefield or when they return home."

For more information about Robin Schmidt and her mission,
visit her website at http://alwayssupportourheroes.com

Ron Kibbey

Former Hippie Serves People of Winchester

He was young, idealistic and believed passionately in a "peace and love mentality" that swept the country in the 1960s. He looked the part, too, with shoulder-length hair, granny glasses, jeans with "real" holes. And, he drove a VW—though not the classic hippie mobile.

"People want to make it a VW bus, but it was actually a Beetle," said Kibbey.

That's important, because long ago, Kibbey's Vermont-bound VW Beetle broke down while on a cross-country trip from California not long after Kibbey served four years in the U.S. Air Force in a non-combatant role. The car stopped dead with a broken clutch cable, near the old Bonded gas station in downtown Winchester, not far from where his aunt was living.

Fortunately, for people in the Winchester community, Kibbey has been content to be "stranded" there for more than thirty-seven years, and, along the way, has helped significantly change the landscape of human services in Clark County.

His influence has been compassionate and effective. He has helped hundreds, perhaps thousands, to raise their standard of living and improve their lives and families—and, for many, to achieve their long postponed dreams.

Interestingly, except for being thirty-six years older, he still looks a lot like the hippie of the 1960s, except that he now commands respect even among the most staunch conservatives in town. Truly, his ideals have not changed, either.

Ron Kibbey

Kibbey began his Winchester career as a social worker in December, 1973, shortly after the car breakdown. "I had to have the VW towed to Lexington," he said, "because no one worked on foreign cars in Winchester at that time."

While staying with his aunt in town (the purpose of his visit to Winchester), he wandered aimlessly into the employment office while killing time and casually asked, "Do you happen to have any jobs working with people?"

A lady at a desk answered quickly. "We just happen to have a social worker position becoming available this Friday. You might be qualified, but first you'll need to take a test in Frankfort."

The hippie soon was hired as a social worker in Winchester, Kentucky—a long way from Vermont. Kibbey never regretted the decision. He became a fixture in the town where people love Ale-8-1 soft drinks and are passionate about favorite-son film-maker Jason Epperson.

To this day, Kibbey has a mantra that guides him, one he developed as a youth growing up in a blue collar neighborhood in Baltimore, Maryland. It is one that followed him when he graduated in 1969 from Towson State College (now Towson University). A mantra that guided, even, his work in the Air Force.

"I believe anybody can change, can accomplish ... become self-sustaining," Kibbey said, "if we can help them to remove barriers that prevent it from happening."

An example of the barriers he saw around Winchester fairly soon after taking the job was that the local social service agencies were not properly informed about the others' responsibilities—both in terms of what each agency *could do* and also what they *couldn't do*.

"The groups weren't talking to each other and 'turf wars' developed," said Kibbey. "People were working against each other instead of together."

That's when Kibbey and others implemented the idea of inviting representatives from the different agencies to meet monthly. It was simply a matter of better communication.

"We talked about common issues and services," he said, "and we got to know each other on a first name basis."

The Human Service Council was born, and it immediately paid dividends for the community. Kibbey and the council helped develop educational forums where issues such as child abuse, domestic violence, and special education needs were discussed and real solutions began to emerge.

Then a tragic event—the murder of a local child—ignited a firestorm of anger and frustration in the community. "People started expressing how upset they were and many expressed it publicly, and that was it," said Kibbey. "But others participated in bringing some solutions to problems in our community"

Soon, their idea of a "drop-in" day care center called Rainbow House opened in a local church. In 1985, Kibbey spearheaded the establishment of the Latch Key program, which used local schools to provide a safe place, along with positive activities, for children who came home from school and were left unsupervised while their parents were at their jobs. The program is now called Kids Carnival and is still going strong at most of the county's elementary schools.

Kibbey served as president of the Clark County Association for Handicapped Citizens for many years. He, Joe Ann Dove and many others were concerned about opportunities for those with physical or mental disabilities after leaving public school services. That concern led to Camp Clark, a summer recreation and socialization program for the population—one that later evolved into a vocational program.

Now the clinical director of Comprehensive Care in Winchester, Kibbey was on the original boards of the Winchester YMCA and Big Brothers–Big Sisters, and he was a force in forming the Community Services Center, an effort of local churches and government to more efficiently serve indigent citizens.

Dove, who also has an admirable resume of service to the community, praised Kibbey for facilitating a staff that is "constantly at work in the schools, in the jail, at the center, and at the Pioneer House, providing services to the community. Ron is self-forgetting, dedicated, and committed."

Two nurses at the Clark County Health Department echoed Dove's admiration of Kibbey. Carol Hisle, who coordinates the diabetes program there, noted that "Ron is an outstanding individual who seems to always be available in our community to assist on any project, work on any committee while maintaining his professionalism." Karen King, a nurse administrator, pointed to the fact that Kibbey "has a gift of helping others keep things in perspective and see the positives in practically every situation."

In Kibbey's mind, the "positives" that Karen King mentioned are like watching a great adventure film, where all the challenges, the acts of courage, the excitement of new frontiers navigated pay off, eventually, in a triumphant way, leaving the audience with a sense of private joy. "As I see it," noted Kibbey, "we're kind of like Johnny Appleseed, going around with a pack of seeds on our back and sowing them. We don't always have the opportunity to see them grow, but sometimes we do...."

He remembers counseling a high school senior about her future vocation, a young girl living with her family on a tenant farm. Kibbey was warned that "you're wasting your time on her. She'll never make anything of herself." The remark emboldened Kibbey to work even harder with the impressionable youth, helping her get an educational grant to train in the medical field.

"Years later, I found out that she is now a doctor in Florida," beamed Kibbey.

There are the drug abusers he has counseled in jail, who, he says, "want to get clean, and want to change their lives. You see their humanness when you talk to them one-to-one." More time and money needs to be spent on rehabilitation rather than locking people up, Kibbey thinks, as he believes jail is "extremely costly, and they often come back out to get in trouble again."

Some might suspect that Ron Kibbey struggles with a chronic and incurable case of simple naiveté, that he imagines an unrealistic world of "nice" where all will be well if we only communicate and treat others with dignity. He might be easily dismissed for that reason, but for Kibbey, his effective staying power has demonstrated that he's much more than a Pollyanna spirit.

In his years of service, he has accumulated a healthy dose of experience-based wisdom. In regard to the oft-stated admonition to "pull yourself up by your bootstraps," he has some strong thoughts.

"In theory, everyone *can* do that, but what if you don't have any boots?" he asked. "We need to help those people *find* the boots, to help them remove the barriers to achieving for themselves."

Kibbey has learned to work within the often daunting bureaucracy to achieve good results. "The system, I think, is here to protect and give support," he said. "It can also 'trap' people in a box. I have to talk to some and teach other ways to do things than to 'beat the system.'"

Incidentally, his work as an office worker on an Air Force base in the Mojave Desert "taught me a lot about working well in a bureaucracy," he said with a sly grin. Some might say that Kibbey is gifted in that regard, and that he is further fueled by his passion to meet human needs, and to connect.

Grace Witt started her tenure as a nurse at Winchester's Clark Regional Hospital, and she often felt a sense of tenseness. "Ron, as a social worker, was a great resource for me and a person that always had time just to talk and assure me that things would get better and easier," she said. "He made a stressful atmosphere a place of peace when he was around."

For modern day hippie Ron Kibbey, the hours are long, the obstacles are real, and the recent economic recession has made his vocation, and avocation, especially more difficult to navigate. Daily, he faces nagging challenges. But he has no imminent plans to retire. There's too much to do. Naturally, he sees better days ahead and probably always will.

Kibbey was chosen as one of Kentucky's "torch carriers" for the 2000 World Olympics Events, one of his happiest moments.

Unifying people for a greater good, as the Olympics seeks to do, just makes sense to him. In retrospect, Kibbey has always carried a torch for the dignity of humankind.

Now in his early sixties, Kibbey still dreams, and he still hopes. He dreams about helping diminish the stigma of mental illness, an area of specialization for the last twenty years—that those who suffer from the affliction will be treated with more understanding. He hopes to make it easier for the elderly, in particular, to be treated, and he wants to promote education on the issue.

He thinks about how special it would be to see those with prior felony convictions be given more employment opportunities and experience a realistic chance to turn their lives in a positive direction. He knows it can work, and the community will benefit. "We want ex-felons to work, but we don't always want to hire them," Kibbey said of the dilemma.

Kibbey would like communities everywhere to invest in our children, to encourage all to think big and noble thoughts, and to look for the best in each person we encounter.

"We need to accept others where they are," said Kibbey, "and understand that they *can* be someplace else."

Fortunately, a hippie who's wheels stopped rolling in a central Kentucky town back in 1973 is still there. For those who welcomed him, and for the others who embraced him later, it seems the karma was right for this groovy partnership.

Charlie and Elaine Fuerniss

Paris Couple Finds Meaning in Animal Rescue

On one of their first dates, Charlie and Elaine picked up a stranded kitten along a South Dakota roadside. At the time, it didn't occur to them that their act of kindness was an omen for the future.

More than three decades later, Charlie and Elaine Fuerniss pick up, take in, transport and do all manner of good for animals, mostly dogs, and often cats who are stranded. These days, the couple operate their mission of mercy from their small horse farm near Paris. They each have full-time jobs, but even a casual observer would say that their rescue work is full-time, too.

Total immersion into their time-consuming passion is evident when one visit's the farm. The friendly barking you'll hear when approaching the Fuerniss's house, about a quarter mile off the main road, is from thirty to forty dogs. The diversity of sizes, shapes, colors, ages and personalities of the animals make it a sort of rural cosmopolitan setting, a canine community that works well.

"They usually get along pretty well," said Charlie.

The St. Bernard, Beethoven, looks a dead ringer for Stephen King's "Cujo," but Charlie says he's sweet, and he does appear to come in peace. There are puppies of all sorts, but there are the seniors, too. There are the cute and pretty, and there are, well, the ones with needy eyes peering out of homely faces and lop-sided bodies.

Charlie and Elaine Fuerniss

"It's quiet at night," said Charlie. "Loudest time is the feeding, or when somebody drives up. Other times, it gets pretty mellow and everybody chills out."

For most of these lively creatures, the Fuerniss farm is a temporary, but pleasant place to live until someone comes there to adopt, or until Elaine and Charlie get a call to send a few to another home, sometimes to far off states like New Hampshire or Maryland. Others may go to another location in Kentucky, where the animals can be "relayed" to new homes by others in a large support group called United Rescuers of Kentucky.

When people desire to adopt an animal at the Fuerniss farm, they pay to have the necessary health related procedures, like shots and worming.

"It costs about $75 to $100 to get them ready," said Elaine, "and the money goes back into the operation."

Though the couple sometimes take donations to defray costs, they make no profit—only the satisfaction that the animals are being treated humanely. "We don't worry about the money part of it," said Charlie.

On another front, there's Charlie and Elaine's low-cost spay and neutering clinic in Paris that operates on Saturdays, which they opened several years ago.

"We talked to a group in Lexington that was similar, except that they made mobile visits to communities in the area," said Elaine. "They gave us the idea and information we needed to get something going here."

A huge part of the impetus for the Bourbon County project can be attributed to their teenage daughter, Michelle, and her untimely death in 2003 involving a horse-related accident on their farm. Michelle's life inspired others.

"Money had been donated to the animal shelter where Michelle volunteered," said Elaine, who is also a cancer survivor. "The shelter wanted to see the clinic get started."

The couple believe that in many ways, they can see Michelle's influence in their current animal-rescue work, which also was her passion.

At the clinic, several local veterinarians accept lower fees. Other help includes what Elaine called "a nice group of mature and responsible teenagers," along with neighbors and even some volunteers from outside of Bourbon County.

Working together, they have turned the clinic into a good model for meeting a glaring need to keep the animal population to a sensible, manageable number as well as being cared for properly. "The idea with having spay and neuter clinics is to work ourselves out of a job," said Charlie, with a smile.

In many places in the Northeast United States, the problem of neglected and mistreated dogs and cats is much less serious than in

Kentucky. Their spay and neuter programs are widespread and working well—almost too well.

"Some of their shelters are empty," Elaine said. "For those wanting to adopt, they often are on three-week waiting lists."

For that reason, the animal transports from Kentucky are important. The Fuernisses are part of a statewide network of relaying volunteers. "Some of the relay trips are 800 to 900 miles round trip, which we often do in a weekend," said Charlie. "We know a lot of other people who are involved in these transports, too."

He would like to see Kentucky state government become more involved. "I'd like to sit down with someone at the Department of Agriculture and talk to them about the benefits of a good low-cost spay and neuter program around the state, and how it would save money," said Charlie.

A great part of the Fuerniss's work in animal rescue is simply communication. It's a time-sensitive endeavor requiring quick decisions and changes in plans.

"I'm always checking my e-mail, making calls about transports needed to do and adoptions," said Elaine. "You never know when you might have to put a dog in your car and take it to someone else."

A recent day for Elaine illustrates the frenetic pace of the couple's life in service to animal's well-being:

- Off work at the hospital at 7:00 a.m., she checked her e-mails, including one that dealt with a pregnant dog to be transported to Wisconsin.
- Elaine arrived home about 9:30 a.m., then promptly delivered two dogs to Millersburg, a thirty-mile round trip.
- Back to the farm, she soon departed with a kitten on board, this time to a pet shop in Lexington.

o After returning, Elaine slept until 4 pm, arose and hosed down the animal concrete-slab living area, while continuing to take rescue-related phone calls, knowing that she would soon be heading back to the hospital to work her shift.

Charlie's schedule might focus on other points of emphasis, but he is typically just as busy. Besides his job at FedEx, he gives the animals their meds, takes care of ten horses, prepares for a weekend animal transport, and makes time for his wife and him to talk and eat meals together, something that was always important as they raised their three girls. One likely would not be surprised at their main conversation topic.

The couple are active members of the local Annunciation Catholic Church where, "people were so supportive when we lost Michelle," said Charlie. "Thank God for our friends who have helped us."

And a sizeable animal population in and around central Kentucky are fortunate and likely feel the same gratitude toward Charlie and Elaine Fuerniss who help and care for them.

Evelyn Johnson Seals

Writer Opens Home and Heart to Those Who Need

It is a place of hospitality, where human needs are thoughtfully considered. She calls it, simply, "The Blessing House."

Sometimes it's full of basic foodstuffs and blankets; at other times it sits awaiting a refill from a giver. When the goods are available, they lie in a smallish room adjacent to the living room, serving as a mini-warehouse for the poor, or, at least, those who are struggling mightily.

"Giving to others what is given us," said Evelyn Johnson Seals. "People bring us things and we give what we get."

For Seals, her two greatest passions, beside her family, are giving to others and writing. Writing about what she calls "the mountain people," kindred souls she knows from growing up around Middlesboro in the Cumberlands. She writes about people she has met in her travels with her husband, Ken, who is an elder at a Church of God fellowship. "We take one *big* trip a year," says Seals.

She and her husband of over forty years live in a modest, white-framed house which sits on a hillside in town in the hollow where she has spent her over sixty years. It is a short walk to the historical Cumberland Gap. From out of the Seals' home comes a scrumptious meal on Thanksgiving, with as many as 129 people attending—often many people Evelyn Seals has not previously met. Three

31

grown children are fully oriented to this way of life, and they pitch into the effort with vigor. Besides the annual Thanksgiving feast, there is an on-going, but mostly informal program Seals champions. Needy folks call and come by several times a week during the year. Each may receive clothing, or possibly a warm afghan, depending on what The Blessing House has available at the time.

Ken and Evelyn Johnson Seals

The afghans are supplied by an organization called The Warm Up America! Foundation. When pressed for a count of how many of the afghans she has distributed, either from her house or by taking them to nursing homes and other places, Seals says "probably in the thousands. They have a set number of them they send, but they often put extra in with what they ship me."

There's no bureaucracy to deal with at The Blessing House, no cold stares or long waits for approval. "I don't make anybody fill out any papers," Seals said. "If someone tries to take bad advantage of things, the way I see it it's *on them*."

She's been a care-giver for two brothers, both of whom have suffered debilitating mental conditions, and she cared daily in her home for her mother until her death.

Seals is a compassionate and creative spirit, humble and especially happy when she writes. She's authored three books, with *Mist of Memories*, a collection of poetry, in the fourth printing (about 2,000 copies total).

A selection, "I'll Have a Visitor Someday," shows poignantly the empathetic way Seals relates to others who hurt. While visiting what she calls a "home for the aged" in Atlanta, she met *"a little old lady standing in the hall. Her hair was white and her voice was shaking, she told us what she had to say ... 'I'm going to have visitors someday.' ... Her words play on my mind like a record night and day."*

For eleven years, Seals wrote a column for the *Middlesboro Daily News* called "Appalachian Moments." "I poured my soul into those columns," she said. She can relate to the daily hardships and the deep-seated loyalty to family kinship that is a hallmark of Appalachia. In a column devoted to her deceased mother, whom she lovingly refers to as "Queen of Hearts," Seals remarked that Mother *"has found the freedom of eternity. I can only hope so in order to keep my sanity."*

The passions of giving and writing seem to have formed together early in Evelyn Seals's life. Her parents were givers, and her father, especially, was a reader. "My dad was Ulas Johnson, a Pentacostal minister. He died in 1961, as he lay on his bed with tuberculosis, he had his books all around him. I read each book. I was first published when I was about thirteen in something called *The Herald of Hope*. I *have* to write."

Seals sums up her work by saying, "That's my love—telling about the people here and then doing for them."

Besides establishing The Blessing House, Seals counseled Alcoholics Anonymous members for fifteen years. She's met with inmates in jail and she's helped military veterans. One time a week, Seals drives out to another hollow in the county to check on and bring food and other provisions to a person who is disabled.

Though Seals shuns looking for accolades, she has won a local "Woman of the Year" award three times, and was named "Volunteer of the Year" in 1999. She's received numerous recognitions from the Disabled American Veterans for service, and was once featured on a TV program originating from New York called "America's Talking." Afterwards, she was rewarded with a sum of money in support of The Blessing House.

Bobbie Warf, sister of Seals who has also worked with her on many of the projects of compassion, says: "All the things Evelyn Johnson Seals does are not for publicity. She simply sees a need. She was raised in poverty and has spent her life giving to others."

Over a decade ago, Seals suffered a stroke. Later, she fell and broke an ankle, and she spent time in a wheelchair and with a cane. Giving in the Seals household didn't cease, however. Her relatives, including her three grown children and husband, "kept things going," said Seals, who also has six grand-children.

For the future, she hopes all three children "will want to do something like this." Looking ahead in the short-term, Evelyn Johnson Seals, now in her mid-sixties, would like to continue her ministry of compassion. She grinned when she remarked about her husband's part in the endeavor. "When I go to ask him something," Seals says, "he says 'What have you volunteered me for now?'" Also, she'd like to write another book.

"I want to do a book about the hollow I was raised in," she says.

Her book will likely be a strong testimony of the influence of doing simple acts of love which have made hundreds of lives better—a fitting tribute to her kind-hearted ways.

Dale Faughn

Octogenarian Educator, Poet Lives Young

It doesn't occur to the energetic Dale Faughn that only a young person might arise from bed at 3:30 a.m. and jog three miles—all before going to work.

He doesn't consider number of years lived as a negative criterion for being a blood donor, as the more than twenty five gallons he's given at his regional blood center and other places attest. Faughn still hungers for more knowledge to improve his teaching skills, honed over a career-stretching sixty years. That's why the science teacher continually travels the country attending professional development activities.

And, all along all the path Faughn trods, his simple love of language and experiences are expressed publicly through the avenue of poetry.

Pretty impressive for anyone, and especially an eighty-four-year-old man.

Faughn teaches science at Caldwell County High School in the western Kentucky community of Princeton. He plans to stay there "until I get old," he said, "or until the custodian finds me dead sitting at my desk after school."

It's not because he's trying to set some kind of record for career longevity, but because he loves his profession, and he's very good at it. Faughn has garnered a multitude of recognitions for his classroom work, including induction into the National Teachers Hall of Fame, and he has won a prolific number of state-wide education awards, including Kentucky Teachers Hall of Fame.

Dale Faughn

The slightly built, 137-pounder shared the honor of 1986 Kentucky Poet Laureate with Jim Wayne Miller, and he uses his poetry skills frequently in his classroom. Entirely in tune with the needs of his community, Faughn was inducted into the Baxter Donor Hall of Fame for his work in giving blood. He won "Citizen of the Year" from the Princeton Kiwanis Club and has long been actively involved in churches around his hometown of Fredonia.

"Don't be ordinary," says Faughn.

And oh, what interesting—and true—stories he tells about himself. Like the time in 1958 when he became a national TV personality for a short while.

"I didn't tell anyone that I was applying," said Faughn, "but I filled out the papers to be on a TV show called "The $64,000 Challenge." He heard from them fairly quickly. "They asked me a lot of questions on the phone about my Bible knowledge, then flew me to New York City for the program. Before going, a store here in Princeton stayed open after hours to help me get the right suit to wear." Supported by his surprised family and community, Faughn performed well on the program but eventually was defeated by "a very nice lady who really knew her Bible well," he recalled. His consolation prize was a check for $8,000. "A lot of money at that time," he noted.

Faughn often relates stories of his Depression-raised youth to his wide-eyed students, amazed that their teacher's father was a sharecropper and a farm hired hand who worked from "sun to sun" for fifty cents a day in wages. Faughn tells that he was drafted into the U.S. Marine Corps and departed on a cross-country train trip to San Diego for basic training just after he graduated from Eddyville High School, in Lyon County.

"We were poor, and I didn't get to go anywhere until going into the Marine Corps," Faughn noted. Working hard in school was important in his family. "My parents always pushed education and I hungered to read and to learn."

On the way to San Diego, he took notes as he viewed the countryside. Returning from Iwo Jima, he wrote his first poem about the place, called "I Met the Flag at Iwo Jima." He still likes to dress, occasionally, as Uncle Sam for patriotic poetry recitals he gives.

Later, Faughn took advantage of the government's GI Bill of Rights to attend college at Murray State. It was a godsend, a cherished dream for him. Faughn grins when he tells of his austere living style while there, influenced by his vivid memories of living in Depression times.

"My tuition, books and fees were paid. I was given $50 per month to live on, but since they ran out of dormitory space, Murray State found me a place to stay for $7 a month, and I spent $1 per day to eat, plenty. I had $13 left at the end of each month after room and board."

Faughn's ability to handle finances allowed him to establish an annual $1,000 college scholarship award, in tribute to his own parents and maiden aunt, at Caldwell County High School for a deserving student who plans to teach.

"If you see a turtle sitting on the top of a fence post," Faughn likes to say, "you can know it did not get there by itself. I am grateful for all those who have helped me along the way."

A big part of his success, he admits, is through the help of his wife Virginia, who resides with him at their farm near Fredonia, outside Princeton. The couple married in October, 1949, after they met as she worked as a student cashier at Murray State's cafeteria. "There was something about the way she punched my meal ticket," he said with a grin.

She resigned herself to be the wife of a busy teacher. "It hasn't been easy for her, as I was away so often while she was home raising our seven children. I couldn't have made it without her cooperation." Six of the seven children were boys, and only one of the seven chose education as a career.

Virginia's passion is to minister to the ailing in the community. "If someone is sick, Virginia knows just what to take to them," said Dale. He likes to travel; she likes staying around home.

"Being different has worked well for us," he said.

Dale Faughn has a work attendance record that borders on the outrageously positive side. "As best as I can remember," he said, "I have used only thirteen sick leave days in over 60 years. I make myself go. I missed eleven of those days when a dog ran out in front of me on my bicycle and I broke my hip."

Besides his regular physical exercise regimen, Faughn attributes his good health to taking vitamins, minerals and avoiding caffeine, alcohol and tobacco. "I don't feel old. "It's not age that makes the big difference, it's the way we perceive age," he said. "I've had 'old' people in my classes."

Faughn's guiding mantra is to be "never satisfied" with what he seeks to accomplish. One of his seven books of poetry is even named *Don't Be Ordinary*.

"I'm not one who just likes to 'glide through,'" he said. "I sometimes struggle with having patience, though."

That issue may be well reflected in how he runs his science classes. "I like to keep things moving, change activities. I write songs and poems to use, and I ask the students to express their feelings through short writing activities. Lecturing has its place, but that is only one of my teaching techniques."

Faughn's books of poetry, illustrated by his good friend Ricky Phelps, are both products of his passion to express his astute life observations and a need to encourage many people, not just the highly literate types who look closely for hidden meaning in poetic writing.

"I write my poems so that anyone can understand them," he said. In a piece called "Forget the Birthdays," Faughn does just that in his last stanza:

> My message is simple:
> Don't wilt up and die;
> Don't cower in slavery
> To birthdays gone by.

Dale Faughn simply has never made his age an issue in anything he's ever done. This vibrant and kind-hearted man, a born teacher and consummate man of letters, would rather write you a poem for your birthday than to send you a store-bought card.

Because of his overarching authenticity, Faughn's legacy will be something like this: Always carve out your own individual niche in life—but do it for the betterment of others.

Mary Lou Boal

Travel Agent Offers Comfort to Cambodians and Others

Catching Mary Lou Boal sitting still is a challenge. When caught, getting her to talk about what frantically drives her is *no* problem. If her carefully spoken and uplifting words don't reel you in to her current service project, her easy laugh and animated voice certainly will.

Boal is a real-life mover and shaker who deeply believes in the dignity of all human beings. Fact is, she's a dynamic force for good in her community, both the local community and one existing far away at a place said to be "forgotten by the world."

Madisonville is her long-time home, but it's really only a nice refueling station for this vibrant sixty-eight-year-old. Boal arranges international traveling experiences for her clients through her Total Travel Service Agency. She has taken people on tours to seventy-five countries since she started the business in 1982.

One country, far more than any other, has captured her imagination and ignited a passion for its fourteen million Asians—that being Cambodia. Enough to motivate Boal to go to near-heroic lengths to bring aid and comfort to the people of this war-torn, poor and struggling nation that has a disproportionably high number of youth and women as a result of the influence of the horrible Khymer Rouge bloodbath regime in the 1970s. And sadly, a nation that averages one in 350 of its population suffering the loss of a limb—due to a pervasive network of landmines set over thirty years ago during the time of terrible upheaval.

Mary Lou Boal

It's a problem that still poses a daily threat.

Boal has played an important role in sending over a thousand wheelchairs to Cambodia. And she has supported a children's hospital there. These projects, perhaps, most clearly define her passion. Working through an organization called Free Wheelchairs Mission (http://freewheelchairsmission.org), Boal addressed groups, got her business involved, and spoke to anyone who'd listen to her story of the plight of the Cambodian people, whom, she calls, "gentle, polite and hard-working people who aren't ones looking for a hand-out, but a hand-up."

She further illustrated her words. "While there, I even came across what is known as a 'butterfly restaurant,' where children are paid to collect and release butterflies for money needed for school," she said. Her part in sending the wheelchairs was not only through the money she raised. She traveled to the country with friend Laura Teague to verify that the chairs arrived at the correct destination and were received by the proper recipients.

The two Kentuckians traveled to a place in rural Cambodia where the chair distribution took place. There, they enjoyed a feast of joy.

"It was from no legs to mobility," Boal said. "Each wheelchair was designated for a particular person, and as they received them, they were soon up and running and happy. It took so many people to see that these people got their chairs, and my excitement was seeing it through."

Teague remembers how the two sat through an hour of speech-making by officials, then watched as some recipients crawled toward their chairs—moving forward on primitive appearing, make-shift wooden blocks on their hands. "Many had no legs, one leg, or a leg that didn't work," Teague said. "It was an amazing sight to watch."

Boal's first exposure to the pressing medical needs of the Cambodians came through seeing the operation of Angkor Hospital for Children in Siem Reap, a noble effort to help, but with only fifty beds and under-equipped. She was touched emotionally, and back home in Madisonville began collecting items the hospital could use at the travel agency.

"We've got to help, girls," was her exhortation to her small, but willing, staff. She collected hundreds of used cell phones that, she was told, could be sold for significant cash. That idea didn't work as hoped, but the people of Madisonville supported her plea for funds and the cash received went directly to the hospital.

Boal continues to support the hospital's work and tries to visit Cambodia several times a year or "whenever I can get an excuse to go." She encourages others to join in the supporting of the people of Cambodia by working through the organization called Friends Without a Border (www.fwab.org).

Besides her far-reaching scope in caring for international peoples, Boal has quite a record for energizing local response to catastrophes around the United States. In the spring of 1999, she spear-headed a group called "Helping Hands of Hopkins County, Kentucky," to answer the call of need in the tornado-ravaged area of Oklahoma. When Hurricane Katrina did its horrendous damage in 2005, again Boal led a community effort to fill a tractor-trailer truck with supplies, even securing a volunteer driver and using her contacts to make sure there was a waiting party in the south to receive the goods.

She leaves few details uncovered when she acts. "I am a good organizer," said Boal, "but the Madisonville community has been tremendous in supporting the projects." Her minister at the Madisonville First Christian Church, Rev. Don McLaughlin, described her as "one who has a wonderful heart for mission to help people in need" and "she uses creative ways to find resources and is persistent." McLaughlin marveled at the effect she has on people around her. "Mary Lou's enthusiasm is contagious. She has a natural personality for helping and her motivation comes from her faith," he said.

Teague described Boal as "dedicated, energetic, and compassionate ... an 'Energizer Bunny' who I could not keep up with when we were in Cambodia. She is one, since I first met her, who always has a project she is working on and is always able to carry it out."

The deep well of compassion that bubbles inside Mary Lou Boal may come partly from the influence of her own childhood upbringing, where she was taken in as an infant with open, accepting arms by her father's sister when her mother died. "I was treated as well as everyone else in the family—with plenty of caring. My father was living in Kentucky and couldn't care for an infant at the time. But I had a wonderful childhood," said Boal. She remembers, too, about living next door to a church parsonage and being aware of international missionaries, many who were not Americans, who often had Sunday dinner in her house. "I saw the good treatment and respect shown them, and I still see the image in my mind today," she said.

Tom Clinton, editor of Madisonville's daily newspaper, *The Messenger*, describes Boal as "tireless ... and she knows how to utilize the media to accomplish her goals to help others—*and she doesn't fail*. She always seems to look on the bright side and she has the energy of a person half her age."

Mary Lou Boal is Madisonville's "ambassador of caring to the world," a name that is well-earned.

Ann and Chester Grundy

Couple Seeks to 'Make the Race Proud'

She grew up in the 1950s, a "daddy's girl" of a celebrated preacher of a historic church, a place where great music and mighty oratory filled the house of worship, and where luminaries like Nobel Peace Prize-winners Martin Luther King Jr. and Ralph Bunche were not strangers.

Young Ann Beard thrived in Birmingham, Alabama's 16th Street Baptist Church, pastored by the Rev. Luke Beard, where, she said, "people looked out for others and they helped 'make the race proud.'" Some called the place of worship "The Silk Stocking Church" because of the many up-and-coming successful blacks who worshipped there.

Chester was raised in Louisville, son of a World War II military veteran who kept a full-time job and several other part-time ones to make ends meet. Though not highly educated, Grundy's parents saw the need for their offspring to receive college degrees, and all three did. Chester, like Ann, was raised in an environment where all individual actions were expected to uplift and improve the conditions of African-American people.

The two were married in 1974. It seemed to be their destiny to join for a higher purpose.

Together, Ann and Chester Grundy have devoted their lives to uplifting and empowering other African Americans. Based at their home in Lexington, they educate the young about black history and culture by means of a summer educational camp they call "The Nia Project." The term "Nia" is taken from the fifth of seven principles that define the African-American holiday known as Kwanzaa. Nia means "purpose."

Ann and Chester Grundy

The Grundys aim for the camp to be both intentional and purposeful. The program is mobile, taking research journeys to landmarks of social and historical significance across the United States. In all their endeavors, they seek to remind the community of what they may have forgotten or perhaps never knew regarding their African-American heritage.

They have unselfishly used their individual talents to open doors of enlightenment for others.

Chester's interest in history and cultural education moved him, in 1987, to inspire a small group of UK students to successfully establish the Martin Luther King Jr. Cultural Center at the University of Kentucky. Over the years the Center has sponsored a broad array of high quality cultural and artistic programs featuring lectures, theater, dance performances, concerts as well as exhibits and film festivals. Bishop Desmond Tutu, Maya Angelou, Alex Haley, and Spike Lee are but a few of the many high-profile names who have visited the UK campus under the auspices of the King Cultural Center.

As a natural spin-off of his work with the Center, he became a co-founder of Lexington's popular Roots and Heritage Festival, held since 1989. His office also served as a long-time co-sponsor of UK's nationally renowned Spotlight Jazz Series which for twenty-eight years presented concerts and workshops featuring world-class jazz artists to the central Kentucky audience. The performance history of this series includes a host of jazz luminaries including Dizzy Gillespie, Sarah Vaughn, Sonny Rollins, Wynton Marsalis, Dave Abrubeck, the Duke Ellington Orchestra and many more.

Each of the two has a resume of credentials that makes their leadership and message highly credible.

Ann grew up around gifted and courageous leaders in the church. You might say she was part of "living history." Chester honed his skills by being an effective activist while in college, a period he called "a very challenging time to be a black student at UK. A lot of what I do today has its genesis during my time as a student."

Like African-American college students across the nation, Chester was laying the groundwork for the expanding educational opportunities for hundreds of students who had historically been excluded from higher education.

The Grundys' history and cultural-research camp developed largely from their exposure to a summer program sponsored by the Plymouth Settlement House in Louisville's West End, where the two worked before their marriage.

"It was called an 'African camp' that celebrated our black heritage and was based on traditional languages and motifs," Ann said. "This program was more clearly defined by a co-worker, Priscilla Cooper. From that experience, we became deeply involved in reading, research and traveling to Africa. These experiences transformed our lives."

What Chester learned in Africa influenced his relationship with students while working over thirty-eight years in UK's Office of Multicultural Affairs (formerly the Office of Minority Affairs).

"Chester's love for art, history and culture has allowed him to provide an important dimension in the educational development of his students," Ann said. "He believes that one is not truly educated without being grounded in a positive, enlightened understanding of self."

The college paths the two followed in their youths pointed in different directions. Chester chose the University of Kentucky, but his father, because of the severe challenges it appeared awaited his son there, was surprised and maybe even irritated initially. Chester was allowed to make his own decision, though, with the under-standing that he "would not leave UK without a degree."

Ann decided on Berea College, a smaller school that was a bit more minority friendly—though not without the typical race obstacles of the 1960s. "It was not unusual for a white student to resent having a black roommate," she said.

It was while a student at Berea College that Ann participated in a landmark event in America's history—the march from Selma,

Alabama to the capital at Montgomery on March 24, 1965, to protest civil-rights violations and to champion the right to vote.

"We were there to support Dr. King and human rights," said Ann, who traveled with a racially integrated group of students. When they arrived, they joined the action. Walking for miles on gravel and hard pavement was not easy. "I didn't even have a pair of tennis shoes," she said, "and I remember that the shoes I wore were muddy."

Along the way, Ann instinctively used her musical talent to lead other marchers in songs of hope for the struggle ahead. It was an exciting time, a dangerous time—and a time for the ages. The inspiration of her youth experiences at 16th Street Baptist Church emboldened her. She gave an inspirational message to her fellow activists on the bus after the march about the historical significance of what had just taken place. She continues to instill hope and encouragement today as she speaks to various groups in the community about being an agent for positive change.

Chester remembers entering UK in the fall of 1965. "I was looking for a school with ROTC because I had a family that had a strong military background. My ambition back in 1965 was to make a career as a military officer," he said.

He felt alone and not in a hospitable situation at UK. "UK had maybe fifty black students at the time," he recalled. Instead of leaving, Chester threw himself into making a tough situation better for both himself and others. He became a member of the fledgling Black Student Union, and his participation was definitely proactive.

"We were losing maybe sixty-five percent of the students in the first year," he said. "Just atrocious. So the BSU started talking about things such as financial support, the hiring of black faculty, the importance of counseling and mentoring and the necessity of creating an environment that affirmed what we were. We ran a six-week prep course in math and English."

Improvements at UK did come, "but it should be remembered that these changes were largely championed by a small group of visionary students," said Chester. "We were, in fact, doing the work of the administration without financial or other support. We did it because we were determined to improve our circumstances and the future of those who would follow us."

The soft-spoken activist related how he grew deeper in knowledge and appreciation of the black experience during those formative years at UK.

"While a freshman, I met my first true intellectual, an older graduate student who was extremely well-read and had a knack of stimulating lively discussions while we sat together in the Student Center grill," he remembered. "I would always just sit and listen, intrigued by his knowledge and his logic."

The debates about the issues of the day ignited Chester, propelling him toward deeper reading of current events, history, culture and literature—and strong personal growth.

"Sometimes I would read through the night, books by people like James Baldwin and Richard Wright," he said. "Over time, I felt more empowered, more whole. With that knowledge under my belt, it was much easier for me to deal with a very alienating environment that characterized UK in the 1960s."

The highly successful Roots and Heritage Festival originated in the late 1980s as the result of a kitchen table conversation at the Grundy residence. Present with Ann and Chester was an activist who had seen cultural festivals thriving around the country. The talk was full of optimistic yearnings, and soon, Chester Grundy drew up a "vision paper" for the Lexington festival.

"It was presented to Mayor Baesler, and he earmarked $10,000 for a festival—provided the first keynote speaker be Alex Hailey, renowned author and biographer of Malcolm X," Chester said.

With the help of many others, the first Roots and Heritage Festival happened in 1989. "It started with three to four thousand people, and it created a buzz," said Chester. "The second year, the weather was better and the attendance almost doubled." In more recent years, the event has drawn as many as 40,000 people. Chester referred to it as a "magnificent success, a wonderful cultural celebration—peaceful with nobody ever arrested for hurting anybody."

The Roots and Heritage Festival has served to "make the race proud"— like Chester and Ann Grundy had hoped.

The study and travel model for Nia that the Grundys champion is a very disciplined program that typically works with about thirty students. Scrapbooks and personal daily journals are maintained, providing a framework for reflective thinking. Students have to agree to tight, though reasonable rules, including not bringing items that distract from the focus of the trips. In short, the Nia Project is an agreement to learn together. It is purposeful, enjoyable, communal, memorable and life-changing.

Ann remembered a special teachable moment on a trip to Montgomery in the 1970s. "We showed them a film about Bloody Sunday on the Edmund Pettus Bridge in Selma, Alabama. We timed it so that it ended as we approached the Edmund Pettus Bridge (where marchers led by Martin Luther King confronted law-enforcement officials on March 9, 1965). Students and counselors were all in tears," said Ann. "The Nia Project brings tears every year as students stand up to read and share from their journals. They say they have never had such experiences."

As nearly always happens when the Grundys get involved, The Nia Project was rooted in earlier, powerful experiences. The African camp at the Plymouth Settlement House gave them the idea of inviting kids to their home and doing things of lasting value on the local level.

"We documented the history of New Zion (near Lexington), a historical community of enslaved Africans," said Ann. "The church there allowed us to interview their members. We also studied the gravestones at the church cemetery."

Many of the participants for the project came from the Chestnut Street YMCA in Lexington's inner city. "We focused on knowing these students' families and earning their support. This was key," Ann said.

Ann likes to call the mobile camp that developed from research while traveling "a university on wheels. I love the program!" she said. "On so many levels, it works. We train the adults and they are as anxious as the kids."

"We have had boys who probably didn't buy into it at first, but combining travel and exciting study is a powerful combination," Chester added. "When learning is creative and relevant, all sorts of incredible things can happen."

The Grundy household is replete with both African artifacts and personal memorabilia. These special reminders are of a precious ancestry and their fierce, noble struggles. Those reminders, and the people they touch, invigorate them daily as the two continue to do all they can to make the race proud.

Judy Hensley

Inspiring Esteem in Students and Community

When Judy Hensley starts talking classroom projects, she doesn't need to suggest topics. Her students take care of that through their own initiative. She just sits back and watches the students' enthusiasm spill over, often into issues involving their local community—and sometimes even further.

Hensley has faith in her pupils at Wallins Middle/Elementary, enough to move mountains, or, rather, to keep mountains *from* being moved. It's been about a decade ago that her class of seventh and eighth-graders in the Harlan County school got word that nearby Black Mountain, which stands the highest in Kentucky, was slated to be "scalped" by a process commonly called mountain-top removal, whereby a coal company simply blows off the top of a mountain, then procures the exposed coal.

Though the practice has both supporters and non-supporters in Appalachia, Hensley's class took a definite stand against it after first receiving word from a classmate. "A little girl who was very shy had me read her letter to the class," said Hensley, "and the words basically said 'Don't blow it up!' It made the other kids wonder why the coal company didn't want to save the highest mountain in the state."

A firestorm of interest was ignited among the students that day. Soon, the momentum for doing something positive regarding Black

Mountain began building. Skilled in watching projects like this develop, Hensley has long been a proponent of the well chronicled Foxfire Method of teaching, which sees the teacher as a "facilitator" of children's self-motivated and self-directed study of topics they find interesting.

Judy Hensley

Typically, her answer to the question, "What project will your class do this year?" gets a simple answer from Hensley. "Whatever they come up with … I'm not really sure yet."

That year, the Black Mountain project became one of the most exciting of Hensley's teaching career. "The class started doing research and then traveled on buses to deliver letters to the Office of

Surface Mining," said Hensley. "It was a field trip to practice freedom of speech."

Rumblings of discontent concerning the Black Mountain mountain-top removal had started elsewhere. "There were others already meeting and talking about it, but it had not made it into the media," said Hensley. "Once the students delivered those letters, a newspaper reporter covered it. AP picked it up. Then bam, bam, bam. The story made it to Ted Koppel's Nightline and even was featured in a book by Barry Slainbaum called *Hope & Heroes*."

The fired-up Wallins students, along with students from Rosenwald Dunbar Elementary in Jessamine County, traveled to Frankfort to speak to a legislative committee. "That school, with teachers Sandy Adams and Barb Greenleaf, got the ball rolling in central Kentucky," said Hensley.

Tom Fitzgerald, representing Kentuckians for the Commonwealth, filed papers for hearings between the coal and timber companies involved along with The Trust for Public Lands regarding the mining issue. It was resolved the way Hensley's class wished.

"It was problematic along the way, but it came to a good resolution," said Hensley. "So about 20,000 acres at the top of Black Mountain was preserved. There were endangered species there such as Indiana bats, salamanders and indigenous plants. Black Mountain wasn't only significant because it was the state's highest mountain, but also because there were indigenous plants and animals not found anywhere else."

In order that her students also understood the democratic importance of listening to dissenting views, representatives from the mining industry came to class and presented their perspective on mountain top removal. One student, grandson of a mining engineer, held a dissenting view from his classmates He later completed studies at the University of Kentucky and has followed in his grandparent's footsteps.

Hensley was pleased with the learning from the project. "It wound up," said Hensley, "being a lesson on many levels—your public rights, your public liabilities, the need to respect opposing views—which nobody could have predicted when it started."

The project culminated with students from Wallins and Rosenwald Dunbar Elementary holding hands at the base of Black Mountain in a giant ceremony of celebration and unity.

Hensley's classes have also been involved in the protection of Blanton Forest, the largest "old growth" woods in Kentucky. A noted quilter worked with one class to craft "angel quilts." Pen pal relationships have been initiated and developed. Another of her classes worked with Berea College students in Bob Smith's "Aging in Appalachia" project. Together, they interviewed senior citizens in Harlan County and produced a DVD of the experience.

Recently, Hensley's sixth grade class published *Mountain Mysteries II: The Unexplained*, a 192-page book of collected "spooky tales" from students' family, friends, and neighbors—a sterling example of the teacher's emphasis on combining community with classroom.

Another class is working on *Mountain Mysteries III: Tales to Tell at Dusky Dark* and "a video about themselves and their place in the world," said Hensley. As always, the ideas were generated by her students.

"Her focus," said Robert Gipe, Appalachian Center Program Director at Southeast Kentucky Community and Technical College, "stays on her students and how to connect their interests, what is going on in their lives, with the curriculum. She has consistently been one of the finest teachers in the country."

Besides the artistry Judy Hensley demonstrates and fosters in her teaching, she is a regionally recognized writer of short stories. She has also authored two elementary level books, *Terrible Tina* and *Sir Thomas the Eggslayer*, the latter of which Hensley calls a "medieval allegory." She is also working on a sequel, and she dreams of someday becoming a full-time writer.

Her teaching experience extends to being a part-time instructor at the earlier mentioned college at Cumberland. Hensley is a frequent vocalist at her church, and remarkably, she finds time to engage in another of her talents as a photographer.

But clearly, Hensley gets her biggest kick—her greatest joy— when her nurturing influence fosters personal growth in a young person. "It's sometimes difficult to uncover the jewel inside a child," said Hensley, "but kids are so much worth the effort. They're just full of surprises."

Ironically, Hensley started her adult work life as an accountant in Chicago, a place where she grew up after being born in Harlan. "I was a number cruncher for a while, but in the back of my mind was always teaching," said Hensley.

She returned to Kentucky and enrolled in Cumberland College, majoring in education. Following a difficult divorce, Hensley then took the teaching position at Wallins, where she has remained.

"Teaching is one of those rare careers where you get to be an artist, a singer, a philosopher and a psychologist," said Hensley, whose interactive style helps create a "safe place" emotionally for each child. "Every person deserves a positive stroke each day and I just do the best I can. There's always an active list of things to be done as a teacher—and it always starts with a prayer."

Judy Hensley is the kind of teacher each of us always wanted in our own classroom. She's one who has a quiet, studied confidence, but prefers to listen rather than lecture. Dignity, fairness, and striving to serve something bigger than herself are her guiding principles. In the process, she inspires.

Brian Huybers

Youth Uses Eagle Scout Project for Flight 5191 Memorial

It's not unusual to hear bad things about our young people today. Some say they're lazy and they don't appreciate the truly important and lasting things, but only that which will gratify for the moment. Some of the most negative critics even predict that our society's future—with all it's challenges—is doomed to failure because of the emerging generation's self-absorption and lack of character.

Meet teenager Brian Huybers. He doesn't fit those derogatory words, those disparaging characterizations.

The people around Richmond, in Madison County, know what good this favorite son has done. They can take you out to Lake Reba Recreational Park and show you the fitting memorial fountain built to honor six individuals with Madison County connections—all victims of the tragic August 27, 2006, Flight 5191 airline crash at Bluegrass Field in Lexington, which claimed forty-nine lives. Folks can tell you that young Huybers played a huge role in making the memorial possible by both helping to design it and steadfastly raising funds to finance the project.

It was over a year after the plane crash, in September 2007, that sixteen-year-old Brian, a long-time Boy Scout, began searching for a project to gain designation as a highly coveted Eagle Scout. He wanted it to be, foremost, one of personal passion.

Brian Huybers

"First, I was just going through possible projects like putting on new shingles or winterizing cabins at a church camp, plus a few other things," he said.

Those ideas didn't really catch fire with Huybers, a Madison Central High School junior at the time. But then he was contacted by his assistant scoutmaster, Whitney Dunlap, who suggested an idea that had been floating around City Hall—to create some type of memorial to those from the community who died in Flight 5191.

That suggestion hit home with Brian, who remembered seeing the "blue buses carrying family members of the victims" in the aftermath of the crash.

Besides Whitney Dunlap's artful skills in being the project coordinator, Brian soon received a great deal of assistance from Richmond city manager David Evans, who worked with Brian and "fountaineer" Russell Sitter to create a design for the fountain. Sitter commented that Brian "had input on every part of the design," which was an 8,000-pound granite fountain showing forty-nine doves headed in different directions—the number of victims—craftily carved into the stone and with sparkling water peacefully flowing over the doves.

Evans noticed early that Huybers would likely be one to persevere in the process. "I know some people right off, and I could tell his dedication to stick to the project," he said.

The cost would be a whopping $27,000, and the soft-spoken, often reserved Huybers would need to go public to ask for financial donations for the memorial. The endeavor would certainly tax the youngster's personal comfort zone. "Asking people for money was the least favorite thing Brian did, but he got better as he started doing it," said Michele Huybers, his mother. He wrote letters of financial request and notes for his "speeches"—that is, with the help of Mom. "I was his editor," she said with a grin.

Brian began a "speaking tour," which consisted of talking to community groups, including his church. With the guidance of others and his own strong desire, he was on his way toward gaining his Eagle Scout, and, more importantly, he would be doing people in Madison County, and beyond, a kind and lasting gesture.

Positive responses from the letters and speaking audiences began to come. After several months, the teenager's efforts brought nearly $7,000, and the city government promised to pay for the rest of the costs.

On August 24, 2008, the memorial was dedicated at the Lake Reba site. During the ceremony, Boy Scouts released six white doves, representative of the local crash victims. A bagpipe played. Each at the gathering was touched emotionally. Brian Huybers stood tall, knowing that his efforts played a significant part.

"I could never have done it without my family's help," said Brian. "They were with me from the start." He also mentioned Evans, Dunlap and Sitter and family members of the victims as extremely important to the establishment of The Flight 5191 Memorial.

Brian's father, Lawrence Huybers, said that at one point, his son was not sure the memorial project would be approved as a viable Eagle Scout project because of its difficulty level. "But I think Brian would have continued on it even if it were not," said Lawrence. "Brian had gotten so involved in it and wanted it to be completed."

Richmond Mayor Connie Lawson noticed, too. "Brian really went over the top with the project," she said. "I'll bet he really feels proud whenever he sees the memorial out at Lake Reba."

And what are the most important things young Brian learned from his experience?

"I learned not to be shy," he said, and that you've got to do certain stuff with a lot of organizations to make money, and you always have to be talking to different people. I was actually surprised by myself."

Dunlap's duties as a scoutmaster have allowed him to get to know Brian Huybers well over many years. Dunlap said that Brian has "really stepped up his life" since he gathered leadership experience with the memorial project.

"Brian has been a 'sleeper,'" said Dunlap, "and for a long time was more interested in his garage band than campouts. But when he got with the Eagle Scout project, he really started to run with it."

Dunlap saw Huybers go from a modestly interested Scout to become Senior Patrol Leader of his troop. "On a recent Scout trail hike, Brian volunteered to stay back with another boy who was suffering from heat exhaustion. He was the most mature Scout we had and he showed a lot of leadership."

Huybers now is enrolled in classes at Eastern Kentucky University and is tackling the difficult challenges of being a music major, "another example of how Brian is showing self-discipline," Dunlap said.

Mayor Lawson added that Brian's work "is kind of what we've come to expect from our Boy Scouts here in the community."

Thanks to young people like Brian Huybers, it should be quite clear that our young people are still being a positive force, capable of some significant accomplishments if given some old-fashioned support and guidance, like from the Boy Scouts.

Roy Pullam

Born Poor, Teacher Inspires Rich Lives

Roy Pullam won't ever forget the nagging discomfort, the humiliation, the desperate nature of growing up in a poor family. Truth be told, he doesn't want to forget because, even in the difficulty of those times, "there was always someone who came along and helped me at just the right time," he recalled.

Those bittersweet memories spurred the middle-school teacher to do wonderful acts of caring for the vulnerable of his Henderson community. And Pullam's leadership inspired hundreds of young people under his tutelage in the Junior Optimist Club to do likewise.

A prolific reader, Pullam always sought personal direction from the words of noted writers to set a vision for his future. His childhood reminded him of the words written by noted American author, John Steinbeck.

"I identified with the Joad family in *Grapes of Wrath*," he said of the fictional Depression-era family that moved to California to seek a better life. "My father couldn't read but he was a story-teller and could do all his math in his head."

And then there was his mother. "We [children] came first. And, if there was anyone sick in the community, she would go visit them," he said. "When she died, it was one of the largest funerals ever in our community."

Now in his mid-sixties and retired from active teaching, Pullam recollects clearly a particular prayer he uttered as a boy living in the small Kentucky town of Providence, in Webster County, where his mother worked many low-paying jobs because his father was disabled.

Roy Pullam

"I prayed for something to eat. We were hungry," he said, "and the next day this truck pulled up in front of our house and brought us a basket of food." The timely gift was from the local Providence Missionary Society.

He noted that his clothes were given to him by the family's church, and that he "was the poorest kid in the school." Classmates ignored him; Pullam's self-esteem teetered near zero most of the time. Not an encouraging world for a young boy to try to handle.

"I often felt shame about the experience," he said. "Other kids thought of me as odd ... and I *was* odd."

But as Pullam grew older and navigated his challenges, he gratefully received assistance from some personal angels like David Middleton, a man who helped him get a college scholarship. Despite the financial help, Pullam noted that "I had to hitch-hike to get to Henderson Community College." He later graduated from Murray State College.

He was mentored by an aging teacher, Vivian Crowe, who once came to Pullam's rescue when another of his high-school teachers humiliated him in front of the class, telling young Roy he shouldn't expect to graduate.

"Mrs. Crowe flew down that hallway to that teacher and told him, 'Don't mess with Roy Pullam. He's mine!'" said Pullam. "And I *was* hers. She gave me books and made me recite poetry. She taught me what caring was all about."

After graduating with a teaching degree from Murray State, Crowe was "the first person I went to see. She gave me dreams," Pullam said.

The benevolent acts of recent and former students at North Middle School, where Pullam taught for most of his over 30-year career, attest that Roy Pullam gave those young lives plenty of dreams to savor, too.

Here's a sampling of the students' work through Pullam's leadership in the service club he sponsored:

- ○ They gathered over 110,000 cans of food for the Salvation Army, along with 8,000 coats dispersed to disadvantaged people.

o The students sent thousands of books to U.S. soldiers and bought them phone cards.

o Club members raised money to put 78,000 pairs of glasses into the hands of medical missionaries.

o They supported Special Olympics events, visited seniors in rest homes, worked on Habitat for Humanity projects.

o Frequent Christmastime visits warmed the hearts of children at the local hospital, and many poor families enjoyed the gifts given by Pullam's students.

o The Cystic Fibrosis Foundation and American Heart Association received over $12,000 from their efforts.

o Over many years, the Riverview School, a local special-needs school in Henderson, benefited by raising a total of over $102,000 by Pullam's kids by doing raffles, fairs and other activities.

Pullam, it bears no argument, lives a life that is clearly tied to the betterment of others. He's been a groundbreaker in initiating programs to solve pressing needs. He started the Henderson Drug Court with Judge Steven Hayden, giving those plagued by addiction a structured, accountable, and highly focused way to break free to a more fulfilling and productive life—and to stay out of jail.

Along with a physician from the Kentucky Health Department, Pullam designed the first regular local program in the state to do a screening for sickle cell anemia. "A simple test that lot of people didn't know about," he said.

Through the YMCA, he helped Dale Osterman start a class to teach third-graders across Henderson County basic swimming skills—a program that's likely saved lives.

Pullam is currently involved in a bicycle-repair program. The repairs are being done by local jail inmates, and the bikes are given to poor kids in the area. "The inmates are excited and are doing a tremendous job," said Pullam.

Through his career, Pullam frequently used his filmmaking skills for both teaching and recording oral history. He produced the anti-drug film, "Fourth Down and Too Far to Go."

And what might be his proudest venture was working with Jim Long to create the Bonnet Film Co., which produced over 600 audio-visual tapes of notable Kentuckians. The work involved Pullam's students, and together they traveled thousands of miles to gather what has become a treasure of oral history. The collection is archived in the Henderson County Public Library.

Pullam also has helped produce promotional videos for local organizations like the Henderson Literacy Association and the United Way.

As one might guess, Roy Pullam's sensitive, loving heart can be quite easily hurt, too. Leslie Newman, a Henderson attorney, former student and admirer of Pullam, recalled a prank that was played on her teacher when she was a senior.

"Some of the smartest boys in our class … decided one day when Mr. Pullam was out of the room to turn [the desks] around. They moved his desk from the front of the room to the back and turned the desks around and let me tell you there was a lot of activity in a very short amount of time," said Newman.

Though Newman characterized the deed as a "prank, not done with malice by any means, but out of mischief," it caused Pullam to cry. "He was so hurt that his students had shown what he considered disrespect … so it made it a sad story in a way because no one wanted or intended to hurt him but the memory of it still makes me chuckle."

Newman summed up Pullam's positive influence as being "grateful to have had a teacher like him, who cared." She remembered fondly how Pullam "followed my success through college and later through law school," and how "he openly and fondly expressed his love for and devotion to his wife, Velma."

Pullam said his marriage to Velma in 1972 was "the best thing I've ever done." And although the couple had no children of their own, "she was like a second mother to the students all those years," he said. "On all those long bus trips, she sewed the kids' clothes and stayed up with them all night when they were sick and barfing." She steadfastly stands behind her husband and his projects today, sharing his compassionate nature.

Karen Denton, mother of Kurt Denton, a former Junior Optimist under Pullam, praised his influence as a teacher and good citizen: "Roy has done so much for all the kids in the Junior Optimist Club, others at school and in the community. He has been a mentor and friend to so many in Henderson County and I certainly appreciate his part in helping my son become the person he is," she said.

Kaylie Hester, a former president of the club, said of Pullam: "I know no one more dedicated or more committed to make our community a better place. He is an inspiration for us all."

Jerry and Sandy Tucker

Couple's Galilean Home Accepts Those 'Precious in His Sight'

Early in their marriage and with little hope for birthing children of their own, Sandy Tucker exercised her imagination.

"Sandy would rock an empty cradle," said her husband, Jerry Tucker.

Sandy also found another positive outlet for her motherly instincts while the two lived in Michigan. She shared her time at a Catholic orphanage. "She was a part-time mother caring for other women's children." Jerry said.

In time, the two devout Christians opened their hearts—and home—in an extraordinarily unselfish way. Today, one can count over a thousand persons to whom they have given new hopes and dreams, perhaps the gift of life itself at the Galilean Home in Casey County, near Liberty. Additionally—and joyfully—"miracle babies" Becky and Jessica were born to Jerry and Sandy along with the adoption of thirty others.

Sandy, who died at age sixty-two of ovarian cancer in June 2007, was the ambassador—some would say the face—of Galilean Home Ministries, located on a twenty-two-acre compound in the heart of Old Order Mennonite country. "She was not afraid of being around anybody," Jerry noted. "Nothing ever bothered her."

Her boldness was exhibited with frequent trips to places like Mexico, Guatemala, Haiti and Honduras to rescue downtrodden children—sick ones, disabled ones, abandoned ones and those victimized by violence. She struggled against mountains of red tape and corruption in government while seeking either temporary or possibly permanent safe havens for the affected ones.

Jerry and Sandy Tucker

"I want children that nobody else wants," Sandy was often heard to say. "I want to please God."

Sandy succeeded much of the time with the support of her very practical husband, a tall, rugged and determined man with a long and heavy beard. He is one who fixes things, deals with tough discipline cases, drives buses and does whatever it takes to keep the noble operation going well.

"I've always been a hands-on guy," he said. "Sandy was always the people person." Now, Jerry also has taken on the reins of people relations that Sandy formerly commandeered.

"I have no choice," said Jerry. "Mom (Sandy) told me as she was dying … not to quit, to never give up." That total commitment to each other, since their marriage in 1963, has been a hallmark of their service. Jerry continues the ministry, but not without a certain amount of daily grieving.

"I feel her spirit around all the time," he said. "Some people say that I'll get over it in time, but I don't want to get over her. She was so much a part of our lives."

Sandy's grave site sits appropriately behind the soon-to-be completed log cabin they had planned to live in together. It sits off in a private setting away from the main buildings. There are beautiful flowers around the grave. There is an idyllic view of the forested valley below. It's a place of beauty, like the couple's partnership.

At any one time, approximately 50 "children" (though many are actually adults who are totally caretaker dependent) live at the Galilean Home. They arrive from all parts of the United States and all parts of the world. The ministry opened in 1984, and the residents receive ample portions of loving care, with plenty of food and attention to their medical needs. Many are educated at the Galilean Academy, a Christian school on the grounds, as well as other student attendees who live in the Casey County community and desire a religious education outside the public-school arena.

A diversity of interesting individuals mark the life and history of the Galilean Home Ministries. People like Abel, from Guatemala, who lost his arms in an accident and uses his toes to write, Elenue, from Haiti, who had to return to her country when her visa expired, but now possesses an artificial leg due to the Tuckers' influence. Then there is Rosie, one of the many people the Tuckers adopted. Rosie is a vivacious, loving lady mentally disabled as a child when she contacted lead poisoning from a can of paint.

With each person rescued by the Tuckers, there's a particular kind of special adventure—almost always some kind of struggle to bring them to Casey County—and more often than not, a very personal victory is won. Korean-born and biracial Weldon is another example, a child who was given up for dead in a Korean hospital, but after a long and circuitous process, became a part of the Galilean Home family.

In the 1991 book, *Precious in His Sight,* authored by Larry and Carol Troxel, Sandy described Weldon this way: *Weldon was born out of wedlock seven weeks premature in Korea ... with multiple birth defects, chronic respiratory condition, cardio-pulmonary arrest and seizures, and an undeveloped esophagus.*

She described Weldon's appearance the first time she met him: *His nose was constantly running, food would come back through his nostrils due to enlarged tonsils, and his hair was more like a shag rug.*

Though Weldon was termed legally blind and deaf, he became an "official greeter" at the Galilean Home, bounding with unabashed joy as he met each visitor.

It is the The Blessing House on the Galilean Homes grounds that is perhaps the most vivid and endearing portrayal of the Tuckers' compassion. A walk through the building shows twenty-one people with profound disabilities, both mental and physical. These persons often lie bedfast, or possibly are wheelchair bound. Many are of middle age, few have verbal skills from which a first-time visitor can extract understanding. A loving staff acknowledges each person's dignity. The inhabitants of The Blessing House are loved; they are considered, as the title of one of the Tuckers' two books fittingly testifies, "precious in His sight."

Another growing part of the Galilean Home ministry in recent years has been the emergence of The Angel House, part of the Born Free Ministry. Here, infants and children of women who are serving time in prison at Pewee Valley outside Louisville, or Otter Creek in eastern Kentucky, are provided a temporary home in an attractive building with nurseries, staffed by qualified paid and volunteer staff. The outreach was recognized in 1992 for a Presidential Award, and the Tuckers traveled to Washington, D.C. to be honored by President George Bush.

The Bread of Life Café, an attractive building on Highway 127 several miles from the compound, became another part of the Tuckers' ministry in 1995. Besides serving full-course meals six days a week, the establishment includes a gift shop. Many of the Galilean Home residents are employees of the ever-growing and popular restaurant which seats 150.

Though the mission of the Galilean Home Ministries never seems to stray from its aim to help individuals meet their needs and to gain a sense of human dignity, the work the Tuckers set in motion has become a rather large business operation. "We require $200,000 per month, minimum," said Jerry, "and we receive no state or federal aid."

The funds, donations of food and supplies, and hundreds of volunteers continue to materialize in support of the Galilean Ministries. Truly, the track record of good works, a well-run operation with good people and the leadership of Jerry Tucker and the abiding spirit of Sandy Tucker attract the best in others. There are 27,000 people on the mailing list. Visitors come and marvel at the mostly self-contained, family-like atmosphere that spells a caring community.

It is a clear miracle for those who don't believe in miracles.

The closeness in the couple that spawned a multitude of kindnesses for others might be summed up in Jerry's words: "Sandy and I were married on January 21, 1963, and for forty-four years we enjoyed the most beautiful marriage I could have imagined … Sandy peacefully left this world for one far beyond description, and there upon the shores of Jordan she awaits me."

She'll no doubt smile at Jerry and say, "You didn't quit."

For more information about the
ministry, visit www.galileanhome.org

Dr. George Wright

'No Excuses' Mind-set Leads from
Projects to College Presidency

When African-American George Wright was growing up in Lexington's Charlotte Court housing project over fifty years ago, he did everything he could to mask what he considered the shame of living in a place for the poor and disadvantaged. He felt increased dismay when his parents divorced. It affected his grades severely, even though he had a good mind. He had the ability to do much better. "I always acted real out-going and was a show-off," said Wright. "I didn't let people know of the hurt in my life."

He received no sympathy from his mother, however. At least the kind that lets one slide by with a free pass because of difficult circumstances.

"My mother taught me there were 'no excuses for not doing well in school,'" said Wright. She also made it clear he *would* go to college someday. "And she told me that if I went around with a chip on my shoulder, people weren't going to help me," he added.

But it took a while before young Wright internalized, then seriously set out to implement his mother's advice. Eventually, her motivating words helped propel him to a sterling career in academia, including the presidency of Prairie View A&M University, in Texas, where he now presides.

Dr. George Wright

Today, Dr. George Wright, armed with his doctorate in history, renowned experiences as a college professor and high administrative positions, along with a treasure chest of hard-won wisdom, gives the same advice to a multitude of eager listeners, and has for many years.

But back to Wright's early years. He remembers the elation he felt when his parents moved from Charlotte Court to St. Martin's Village, which he counted as moving up in status. It soothed his inferiority complex temporarily, but not long after, matters changed negatively.

"My father's drinking began to get worse, causing our family problems," said Wright, "so when my parents divorced, we had financial problems and had to move back to Charlotte Court."

Wright's nagging sense of shame and inferiority followed, and his school performance was poor and his disruptive behavior continued. This happened despite the influence of black teachers, "who gave special caring and encouragement" to students in the segregated schools of Wright's early years, he recalled.

Then, after attending the integrated Leestown Middle School, teenager Wright was given a choice to attend the predominately white Lexington Lafayette High School in 1966, where his older sister was enrolled. The three years there, where he graduated number 391out of 521, were interesting, if not highly successful.

"I was usually the only black in my classes there," Wright said. "In history class, I'd participate in the discussions and people saw me as 'the history person.'" There was a quirk in the young, brash-acting Wright's educational performance, however.

"I didn't turn in many of my assignments or projects," he said. "I didn't see good enough reasons for doing the work, so I didn't. Somebody has to show me good reason to do things, or I won't do them."

Wright graduated from Lafayette High School in 1968 with a 1.89 grade point average. That didn't reflect his ability level at all. But what Wright calls "the most critical thing that happened to me" during that period of life, was an experience he had after getting off work at Lexington's Idle Hour Country Club late one night during his twelfth-grade year.

"When the city bus came to pick me up to take me to Charlotte Court, I saw some of my friends on it," Wright explained. "I did not get on the bus because I didn't want them to see where I was going. I ended up walking a long way home in the cold."

He was demoralized by the events that night. But the experience also served as a game-changer for his whole attitude. "I cried and I cussed," he said. "When I got home, I was done with feeling sorry for myself. I decided then that something had to be done."

After graduation from Lafayette High, Wright enrolled in the University of Kentucky, a place where "people would encourage me in all sorts of ways," he remembered. His performance there was dramatically better, and as he progressed as a serious, hard-working college student, two special persons noticed him while working toward his bachelors and masters degree in history.

One person was his future wife, Valerie Ellison, who Wright "finally got serious with … when I noticed her holding hands with a track star." The two got married while at UK, and "I had a big-time asset as an undergraduate," he said.

Valerie Wright is now a successful journalist who writes for *Texas Monthly* magazine, and the couple have been married over forty years, a union that brought them two children.

Another influential person who saw potential in the re-invented George Wright while at UK was T. Harry Williams, a noted historian who came to UK as a visiting professor. He considered George Wright one of his promising seminar students. Williams wrote a letter to Duke University, encouraging the school to accept Wright into their doctorate in history program. Wright was accepted.

"Duke gave me a three-year full scholarship and gave me $400 per month to live on. It endeared me to the school," Wright said. He received his PhD in history there—and, more impressively, was the first American black at Duke to do so.

With his doctorate from prestigious Duke University in hand, Wright and wife Valerie returned to Lexington. This time, he gained the position of assistant professor at his beloved UK, where he taught until 1980. His style? Hard-hitting and, at times, almost bombastic. His classes typically filled fast, partly because, he said, "I've always let them know they can approach me.

"I've always challenged people, asked lots of questions about their beliefs," Wright said. "I want students to think about things themselves. I challenge black folks to think about race."

In 1980, Wright accepted a teaching position at the University of Texas at Austin where he became a full professor—and very popular. In 1990, he told a class at Austin that he "would be a college president someday." Through his last year there in 1993, he was voted one of the ten best faculty members every year, and, along the way, received the top teaching award at the school.

Wright continued to move upward along the academic career path, joining the Duke University faculty in 1993 to become vice-provost for under-graduate admissions, director of the Afro-American studies program, and held the William R. Kennon Jr. Chair in American History. From there, he moved upward in positions to the University of Texas at Arlington. At UT-Arlington, Wright was executive vice-president for Academic Affairs and Provost, the number two job at the school. He served in that position for eight years.

In 2003, Dr. George C. Wright, who had been an under-achieving student throughout his formative years while growing up poor in Lexington's inner-city, became the seventh president of Prairie View A&M University, near Houston, Texas.

In 2004, Wright was the graduation commencement speaker at UK, where he was presented with an honorary doctorate of letters. It was a tremendous honor, but, ironically, it was also the year that the Wrights' daughter, Rebecca, died—"something that's always on my mind," said Wright. The couple has a teenage son, Benjamin.

Taking his life as a whole, Wright feels like a blessed individual. "It's never been far from my mind—living in Charlotte Court and walking home that night in the cold," Wright said, "I don't know why I had to live like that and I don't know why I live like this now."

George Wright can "live like this now" because of the mind-set he adapted when he first set foot on the UK campus back in 1968—a razor-focus on some high-minded academic goals he had previously ignored while younger. His wife watched as her husband gained success with maturity.

"He really buys into the idea that he is willing to work harder and longer than anyone else. He's up by 5:30 a.m. Monday through Friday," said Valerie. "Since his graduate school days, he has kept the list of Benjamin Franklin's 'Thirteen Virtues' posted in his work area or his study. He tells his students that education made all the difference in his life, that it will do the same for them and, by extension, the members of their families."

Wright admitted: "I'm not that smart. I work hard … and I make no excuses for anything."

Just like his mother told him.

Books by Dr. George C. Wright

A History of Blacks in Kentucky: In Pursuit of Equality, 1890-1980, Volume II, (Kentucky Historical Society; 1992, 2008)

Racial Violence in Kentucky, 1865-1940: Lynchings, Mob Rule, and Legal Lynchings (Louisiana State University, 1996)

Life Behind a Veil: Blacks in Louisville, Kentucky (Louisiana State University, 1985)

Robert Charles O'hara Benjamin: A Forgotten Afro-American Leader (in-progress)

Shirley Donathan

Bath County Lady Always There to Help

Just like most of us, the folks around Owingsville have to deal with everyday challenges. Around the Bath County community, people get sick and need careful attention while some suffer from financial setbacks. Others hurt emotionally, and they simply need a good laugh, a little encouragement or a well-prepared meal to help them get through tough times.

Shirley Donathan was born poor into this world in 1944—one of sixteen children. She has experienced her share of painful difficulties, in spades. Her father was an alcoholic. She left school after the eighth grade to help provide income for the large family, doing jobs like picking blackberries to sell and working in the tobacco crops of neighbors.

Married at eighteen, her first husband was shot and killed by an assailant. She's had a daughter die. Recently a younger sister passed. Donathan serves as a caregiver to her present husband who requires an oxygen tank for breathing. She, herself, survived a bout with cancer.

But what makes Shirley Donathan so special is that when *others* suffer, Bath County people know who to call. She understands and she cares—and she acts.

"We had a *community day* at my house and my sister and I cooked," said Donathan. "We invited anybody who wanted to come, and we had over 200. I just like to do things for people."

Shirley Donathan

And out on Highway 36, the Northside First Church of God is known for their acts of charity. Many of those good deeds are spear-headed by a small group of ladies, called the Fund-raiser Committee, headed by Donathan, who like to cook and like to serve others. It is a ministry that both draws people to the church as well as provides meals for persons in need, such as those suffering job loss, or those dealing with a loved one's death.

"Nobody in the state can cook like these ladies," said Reverend Jim Crouch, Northside's minister. "And people will come as long as they know Shirley is the main cook behind it."

Sometimes along with the group, sometimes solo, Donathan bakes cakes to sell for the benefit of others. Recently, she used her skills to sell thirty cakes for a local high school youth suffering from leukemia, one she didn't even know.

"I was walking through the store (Town and Country Food Mart, Owingsville, where she works) and it was just like God was speaking to me, 'You need to do something,'" she said. The voice Donathan heard may partly have come from her personal experience, at age forty-six, with leukemia. She is a survivor, thanks to a bone marrow transplant from her sister—and her quiet, reassuring, religious faith.

Regarding her trial with cancer, Donathan remarked, "I did great, never was scared."

At the Town and Country store, she is an early morning drawing card for the locals. "She's the reason I have a morning business," noted the store's owner, Jennifer Williams. "She's a good cook and has a great personality. And even after she works her shift, she fills in for others when she is needed."

Donathan takes pride in her participation in Relay for Life, a fund-raiser for the American Cancer Society. For several years, she's been a mainstay in a local horse show done for the organization. "One year, we raised $8,500 and we always did well with it," she said with a glow on her face.

Marcella Doggett, director of Owingsville's Christian Service Center, a thrift store in operation to help low-income citizens in Bath County, told of Donathan's always-willing-to-help mentality.

"She helped a lady who came to us to get transportation to Lexington in order to sign up for some important health-related benefits. She had to be there next day. I couldn't get away to take her but there was Shirley who stepped in to drive her there," said

Doggett. "She (Donathan) won't take any money for it. She follows her heart. She follows God."

But of all the many accounts of Donathan's good works to her community neighbors, there is one that may be most memorable, a story in the year 1999 involving the honoring of a person's "last wish."

"My brother-in-law was dying and he mentioned that before he died, he'd like to visit his sister in Oregon," Donathan said. "I didn't think too much more about it, but for two weeks, he called me and said, 'Are you ready to go?'"

It soon became clear to the soft-hearted Donathan that honoring the man's request was the only right thing to do. So Donathan, her sister, and an ailing brother-in-law with a cancer-ridden body launched what would become a 6,600-mile trip in an already well-traveled van—a van rescued from a junkyard a few weeks before and repaired by a relative.

The journey started in Bath County and headed to the far west coast of Oregon and scenic points along the way. "We took out the back seat to put a bed in for my brother-in-law," said Donathan, "and we took off on a Monday morning."

Because of the kindness of her church congregation the morning prior, her expenses were defrayed in the amount of $372 when a special collection was received.

Donathan let the traveling patient dictate the trip's itinerary. "We saw his sister in Oregon, and then whatever he wanted to do, we took him," she said. "When we got back, my husband looked at the front tires. They had wires hanging out," she said with a grin. "I believe the Lord was watching over us."

The brother-in-law, his request to see his sister honored, died less than a year later. "Other than going to the doctor, he didn't get out of the house anymore," Donathan said.

Shirley Donathan models gratitude, despite living a life that hasn't been easy.

"We struggle," she said, characterizing her own family's financial challenges. But then, she likes to talk about her wonderful brothers and sisters. "I tell you what, I wouldn't trade my siblings for anything in the world. I feel like I'm the richest person in Bath County."

If wealth is measured in respect others have for another, Donathan is abundantly rich. Ronnie Martin, a customer of the Town and Country, summed it up. "You can't say anything bad about Shirley."

Bill Gordon

Naturalist Teacher 'Just Wants to be an Example'

Bill Gordon went green long before it became trendy to do so—more than sixty years ago, shortly after he was born on Christmas Day in 1945. He learned to love the land and appreciate the critters who lived there when he was a youngster growing up in rural Pennsylvania.

Nurtured by his father's love of hunting, fishing, and sail boating, young Bill inherited an adventurous spirit and a keen desire to experience things. He also developed a need to share those experiences with others.

Today, Bill Gordon is the executive director of High Adventure Wilderness School, a highly mobile, individually customized outdoors adventure and educational non-profit operation. It has as its base 500 rugged, hilly, and beautiful acres of a mostly wooded area in Menifee County, just east of the town of Stanton, in Powell County. Gordon is a tall, well-built man with a reddish pony tail who speaks with a clear, almost academic-sounding voice. He pretty much does his passion without any regular employees.

Gordon has a lot on his plate when you consider that he works as a sales associate at Joseph-Beth Booksellers in Lexington four days a week. He has a house in Lexington where he stays during his work schedule, but then, on Wednesday night, he heads east in his old pick-up to his ponderosa in the forest where he'll happily nest until Sunday comes around. The flexible bookstore management has allowed Gordon occasional time off to do his adventures out of the area, such as canoeing with a group in the North Woods of Ontario, Canada, a place he's led those seeking exotic adventure since 1989.

Bill Gordon

Besides taking groups to Ontario, he can also be found teaching his love of wilderness canoeing on various rivers and lakes in Kentucky, Michigan, and Florida. He teaches shelter-building, topographic map-reading, and the cooking of food that's been dehydrated or taken along the way. On other occasions, he sails with participants on the Chesapeake Bay, the Florida Coast, the Bahamas or British Virgin Islands.

At the bookstore and other locations such as schools and community venues, Gordon is spreading the gospel of the outdoors, acting wisely to preserve or improve it. Aptly titled "Wild Bill's Wilderness Workshops," the educational events are attended by both children and adults. Workshop themes cover a wide range of environmental subjects and wilderness know-how.

A few recent topics include bats and bat house construction, basic survival training, gardening for kids, bluebirds, Kentucky wildlife, dehydrating foods, screech owls, fire-building, and basic canoeing. With his deep knowledge and uncanny ability to paint colorful word pictures, Gordon turns group excursions onto his property into hands-on science and history lessons.

"I want people to enjoy the outdoors," said Gordon. "and, although I want people to try difficult things that take them up to the edge of their comfort zone, I'm not looking for them to say 'I survived a wilderness experience,' but rather 'This is great, what's next?' I want them to come back for more."

Walking the trails or tromping the brush around his land with his participants, Gordon likely will talk about a pioneer settlement he discovered with the cabin foundation in place. He may stop and give perspective to the appearance of a snake that slithers by the explorers. Always, his born teacher instincts take over.

"Snakes aren't dangerous unless you attack them. The average person thinks that a copperhead will chase you down and get after you. Unless they're in my yard, I just let one move on."

He talks proudly of the water holes he's dug to attract deer and other wildlife, the bat houses he's built and hung on trees around the property. He'll tell visitors about the grant money, because he has a non-profit organization, that he's used to make his land more nature friendly and self-sustaining. Things like projects he's done to halt erosion, repair logging damage and habitat destruction from previous generations.

"Ever since the pioneer movement started west, we have systematically cleared forests, farmed our topsoil away, filled in swamps, drained off the land and planted exotic species of plants," said Gordon. "We've tried to get rid of all predators, which are things we are afraid of, and things we don't understand. We've done our best to burn, bury, trap, shoot, cut, bulldoze, poison, and run over our world trying to civilize and domesticate our surroundings."

Gordon sees value in going the other way.

One essential element is water, and he's made eighteen various types of ponds, wetlands, and watering holes. He has cleaned up old dump sites and restored logging roads, making thirteen miles of hiking trails in the process. The whole ecology of the area improves with regeneration.

"One feeder stream here was dry most of the year when I first bought this property," said Gordon, "and now it runs clear and has a variety of minnows and aquatic life along its length."

Planting trees, removing exotics, putting up nesting boxes and living in harmony with the land make it an inviting place for wildlife. "This is sort of like a nature field of dreams," he said. "If you build it, they will come."

Gordon beams in praising the good food readily harvested from the woodlands or his garden—but, often a hard sell to his wildlife pupils.

"One of the hardest things for people to do is to try new foods," he said.

Gordon, like others, experienced the well-publicized ice storms that abused Kentuckians in the last few years. But he, unlike most, lived fairly routinely during the time of no electricity and no heat. He had both because he uses his own power generator, sheltered in a small outbuilding near his self-built cottage, and he burns wood in his stove. He need not call a plumber because he keeps a tank of fresh spring water and he has a compost toilet, using sawdust rather than water for waste removal. He is developing a solar- and wind-generator system to feed power to his battery bank.

Gordon is clear about where he stands on the issue of compost toilets. "Septic tanks are not good," he said, "I will always have a compost toilet, no bad effect on the environment. So much of our water is wasted being flushed down commodes so many times a day."

Not a fun subject to discuss, but pretty honest stuff.

But don't think of Gordon as an angry environmentalist who aggressively fights, or protests publicly for change—but also polarizes others in the process. "I feel like I have something to share," he said, "but it doesn't do any good to get mad about things like I did when I was young. I just want to be an example for others, that they'll see some good things going on and they'll want to do it, too."

Gordon has a gentle, precise way of conversing with people about his love of nature. Perhaps unwittingly, he carries an aura of mystique and exudes a deep sense of wisdom that draws people. He is well-read and a 1968 graduate of Penn State University, where he was in the first class of a new environmental studies program.

Gary Cremean, the bookstore general manager, remarked of Gordon's natural ability to thoughtfully engage store customers in a conversation about books.

"Bill, along with another employee, Cindy, always does well in sales competitions at the store," he said. "Bill has a way of leaning down toward people as they speak, and he always keeps the customer in mind and he relates well to the children and others who come to the workshops."

A sampling of courses Gordon teaches, all intentionally made affordable, include ones on "evening" and smooth water canoeing, wilderness training with plaster casting of animal tracks and reading topographic maps, plus basic survival training. Much of Gordon's content comes from what happens to appear in the outdoors at a particular time. A bird with an unusual mating call, for example. The shed skin of a particular snake. An interesting looking mushroom. Is it edible? Why does it grow well here? All are fodder for Gordon to use in sharing a bit of his knowledge with an interested audience—not lecturing, but generously enriching.

Sally Evans, a participant on his wildlife trips, remarked, "Bill has gotten me engaged in the outdoors in different ways. He has quite a 'rapport' with wildlife. He helps me feel more enabled in my own relationship with being in the outdoors." Lexington Parks and Recreation member Lindsay Feazell talked about Gordon's "calming and patient" manner with kids. "We used power tools in some of our workshops with Bill, and he was so careful and patient with the kids," she said.

Gordon draws from a strong resume of personal experiences for use in his wildlife school work. After college graduation, he taught school in northeast Ohio for six years, largely integrating environmental education into regular classes, and working with poor students, both from rural and inner-city areas.

There, while married, he owned a farm and turned it into a modern-day homestead.

"It was the [era] of the *Mother Earth News* magazine, Earth Day, and Arab oil embargoes," said Gordon, "and we tried our best to live a wholesome, rural life. Many of my friends and neighbors were Amish, and they taught us a lot. They would sometimes joke that we were more Amish than some of them. We were green and didn't know it because that term wasn't invented yet."

91

During that time, Gordon, then married, embarked with his wife on a sailboat journey lasting two years.

"We started in Lake Erie, from Cleveland," said Gordon, "and we sailed to Buffalo, New York, where we crossed the Erie Barge Canal to Albany. We sailed down the Atlantic Coast toward Florida, then to the Bahamas. Aside from my love of sailing itself, we got to meet some really neat people, both from here and around the world, some who have a profound impact on the way I think now." During the second year, the couple carried both their two-year and four-month-old daughter on the voyage.

One might ask how the two financially supported themselves during that year. "You can live pretty cheaply on a boat," said Gordon, "and we ate something from the water every day."

Of the trip, many of Gordon's relatives scoffed at the idea. "They told me that it was irresponsible, that these were the income producing years—and that I should wait until I retire to do something like that."

But then he sought advice from his mother on the sailboating trip. "She said that I should go sailing then, that if I waited until I retired, I'd end up just going to the Grand Canyon on a tour bus," said Gordon, "and I never forgot what she said."

Today, as always, Bill Gordon has the practical skills, the intelligence, experience and the energy to make lots of money, drive impressive cars, and live in an upscale neighborhood. While certainly not judgmental toward those who do, he's not interested in those attainments for his own life. He prefers to cultivate, nurture, and show others that each of us can enjoy and appreciate the good earth and the living things that inhabit it.

For Gordon, being green has, and always will be, an authentic way to live his life, and to show others the joy of it.

Fanestia Massey

Uplifting Others after an Unthinkable Loss

For most parents, the foreboding dread of the unthinkable happening, the nightmare of losing a child, is only hypothetical. We usually believe it happens to someone else, not us. It is certainly sad to hear; we even often deal with a short-lived moment, possibly a season of remorse, but then our life proceeds pretty much as before.

Fanestia Massey knows the awful reality and the horrendous, sinking feeling that came from the news that her youngest child, Preston, had unexpectedly died. She knows how it feels to carry a gigantic hole in her heart, nagging her every waking moment, a sort of perpetual grief.

Consequently for many, it's enough of a punch from the ugly side of life to make one bitter, to cause one to withdraw into a protective cocoon, much like dying a slow death themselves.

But for Fanestia Massey, taking that course of action just wouldn't do. It's not part of her makeup. And though it's monumentally difficult, she chooses to be positive and to help others benefit from the pain she and her husband experience.

It was "Project Graduation Night" at Caldwell County High School in the western Kentucky town of Princeton, on May 22, 2004, a day after the seniors graduated. A community effort spearheaded by involved parents, it provided a hoped for "safe haven" for students in the post-graduation ritual that too often across America has resulted in tragic death—the consequences of driving under the influence of alcohol. Parents Fanestia and Roy Massey were present, enthusiastically doing all they could to make the evening a joyous occasion for their son and his peers, and doing it without students using intoxicating drinks.

Fanestia Masssey

Fanestia talked about the events of the evening and the following morning. "There was a large turnout of kids because we did fun things, like jello wrestling, and we gave kids the chance to play games and win money and stay there all night," she said.

"When it was about over, Preston talked about how he had had the 'best time of his life.'" But about 6:30 that morning, the now sleepy Preston decided to drive home while his parents stayed at the school and helped clean the facilities. Some fifteen minutes after Preston drove away, Fanestia and Roy also departed the school, not knowing their upbeat frame of mind would soon dramatically change.

"The accident happened less than a mile from home," Fanestia recalled. "My first words when I saw it were 'Oh, my, it's Preston.' "Before Roy got our vehicle stopped, I jumped out. It was bad. They weren't supposed to but they let me ride in the ambulance. I did not want to leave my child."

At the hospital, the sad words—that Preston had died—were gently spoken to Fanestia and Roy. With the crushing news, there was a follow-up question of urgent importance. Would the couple give permission for Preston to be an organ donor?

In those dark moments, Fanestia remembered well the fact that her son had a kind and helping spirit. Preston exhibited that as he had planned to pursue a career as a nurse, a decision he made after he experienced the opportunity of ministering comfort to his dying grandfather.

"Being a donor was Preston's last chance to help others," Fanestia said. Permission was given, and Preston's two corneas were transplanted to two other people within forty-eight hours. A living, physical part of Preston Massey, even in his death, is now providing a better life for them. But there is more.

From an e-mail note to Massey from Sandy Hickey, representing Kentucky Trust for Life, these nuggets of positive information provide some sense of purpose for Preston's death:

> Preston's donation consisted of orthopedic tissues, which are used to hasten recovery in individuals suffering from bone or spine disease or injury. Many bone grafts can

be generated from one tissue donor. In the case of Preston's gift, our donation records indicate the creation of seventy-five bone grafts which are used to perform reconstructive surgery, spinal fusions, and oral surgery. Our records also indicate that all of these grafts have been distributed for surgical procedures that have enhanced the lives of sixty-two patients thus far. These grafts were distributed to Louisiana, Massachusetts, Pennsylvania, Georgia, Tennessee, Indiana, North Carolina, Florida, Virginia, South Carolina, Arizona, Alabama, New Jersey, California, Illinois, Ohio, Iowa, West Virginia, Kentucky and a medical facility in Turkey. His corneas went to a person in Kentucky and the other in Indiana.

In the aftermath of the tragedy, Fanestia has become a tireless advocate for organ donation, as well as being a vital part of the ongoing Project Graduation at Caldwell County High School. Not only does she expend enormous energy championing these causes, but she's always ready to be supportive of others who experience there own tragedies.

Wendy Fuller of Dawson Springs knows of Fanestia's regard for those who suffer losses. "She has been a rock for many families that have lost their children. She was there when I lost my brother two years ago. We have some friends who lost their daughter and grandson. There was Fanestia, taking care of the family."

Best friend Teresa Cash talked of Fanestia's disarming demeanor as she encourages others to pledge to donate their organs by signifying it on their drivers licenses. "Fanestia never pushes anyone about it. She just uses any opportunity she has to let others know. Her most admirable quality is that she has the ability to relate to any age group," Cash said, also noting the personal inspiration Massey has provided. "I wonder how I would accept something like that happening to me, but she makes me feel stronger about myself."

Project Graduation continues, along with "Preston Massey's Project Pick Me Up," owing in large part to the leadership Fanestia Massey has exerted to go a step further in the aims of the project—to prevent a repeat of what happened to Preston while he drove home that morning. The committee plan by what Massey calls her "wonderful team," developed the next spring after Preston's 2004 death, became focused on a way to have students ride home after the special night in the vehicle of a responsible individual other than themselves.

There was a hitch to the idea, however.

"The committee thought that if the students had to be picked up, they wouldn't come," remembered Fanestia. The thought of renting Humvee vehicles, as a fun, novelty way to get them home safely, was discussed, but the cost was prohibitive. But, the idea that dawned on the group was using plain, unadulterated human nature to resolve the problem.

"We'll pay the kids to not drive home," she remembered saying to the committee. "We decided to have a drawing and have a student win $500 cash, and everybody else would be paid $10 if they were picked up from school instead of driving home."

The parent group, led by Fanestia, soon got busy raising the funds to carry out their Project Pick Me Up. They had their own "jail" project, where notable citizens like teachers and local politicians were "nabbed" and held until someone bailed them. A "singing" with a donation offering was organized at Fanestia's church. One thousand dollars was raised, and the first Project Pick Me Up happened in the spring of 2005, and has continued since. Most students have agreed to be picked up, they've had fun, and they've responded to Fanestia's gentle exhortation that "Preston would tell you to not drive home…"

Preston's comments were always powerful statements to those around Princeton. Preston was popular, was a member of the high school baseball team and was active in his church. "He took his guitar, named 'Grace,' everywhere," said Fanestia, "and his many friends loved to hear it be played."

Fanestia works in the Caldwell County High School office where she has a chance to talk to many people everyday. She doesn't shy away from telling visitors about the good-looking guy on her computer screen-saver, Preston—and his story. She encourages frustrated parents as they walk in the door, telling them to love and appreciate their kids and not fight battles over little things. She understands the important wars that need to be fought, and of the need to chill when it comes to mere aggravations from our young ones.

Massey knows that the sting of Preston's loss will always abide, but hopes maybe, just maybe, a larger miracle will be worked as the lives of others are enriched. "My prayer is that this reaches other counties other than our own," said Massey. "I would also like to encourage everyone to become tissue and organ donors."

Melissa Earnest, an educator and friend at the high school, spoke of Massey's influence: "There is definitely no telling how far she has reached out and touched people, even beyond the borders of our small town and our county. When you throw a stone into a pool of water, the ripples continue on and on and I believe that's what Fanestia has been—a solid rock that has rippled the waters of our lives."

For information regarding Fanestia Massey's "Preston Massey's Project Pick Me Up," contact Massey at e-mail fanestia@mchsi.com. *Information about tissue and organ donation can be found at* http://trustforlife.org.

Joe and June Richey

Couple's Quest Farm Helps Others Realize Dreams

Joe and June Richey were married in 1959 and dedicated their partnership to answering the call of God.

It was to nobody's surprise, then, that they said yes when asked to start a Sunday School class for children with developmental disabilities in their home church, Trinity Baptist, in Lexington. That was in 1960, and the young couple could only dream about what that early act of faith would produce nearly twenty-five years later—that being the establishment of a thriving, combination home and workplace for eighteen mentally-challenged adults, an endeavor that continues today.

By the time the first resident was welcomed in 1984, a whole lot of groundwork had already been done. The project was named Quest Farm, and its planned purpose was clear—to provide a wealth of opportunities for individuals whose lives formerly appeared to be drifting, lacking the wherewithal to gain personal fulfillment because of intellectual challenges.

Quest Farm, as the name suggests, would help people to realize their dreams of living a happy and productive life and become vibrant members of their community. The word "quest" was taken from the lofty lyrics of the song "The Impossible Dream," from the Broadway musical "Man of La Mancha." Residents here, it was hoped, would soar to new heights in following their dreams.

Joe and June Richey

The birth of Quest Farm started, at best, modestly. It would take the Richeys' Biblically speaking "mustard-seed-sized," but power-ful, faith to bring it to fruition.

"The class at Trinity started with just one person," said Joe, "but it soon grew to sixty or seventy, and it kept growing after that."

The ministry for this special population, an almost unheard of program at that time, and, frankly, one not widespread even in public schools, succeeded because many well-intentioned people were involved and willing to work hard at it. Their motivations were similar to the Richeys'—a sense that it was right to do.

"We had about twelve teachers, which included businessmen, school teachers and Gary McComas, the Lexington fire chief," said Joe. "They did a great job."

June, who worked as a special education teacher at Lexington's Bluegrass School at the time, said that a concern developed regarding the church-class members as they aged.

"Parents of our students began to get older and die. We were worried about would happen to our students," said June. And, on the basis of her experiences at the Bluegrass School, June saw community-sheltered workshops as inadequate to meet the population's needs. "Those kinds of work activities just weren't working out."

Joe and June saw a glaring need to provide a program that would help mentally-challenged adults live with a degree of independence and meaningful employment. Their mission was clear, and they were ready to act on what they believed was God's will.

The couple became inspired by an idea from a ranch in Arizona where similarly challenged adults lived and worked successfully. With encouragement from the Arizona director, they set their sights toward developing an operation in central Kentucky. It would be a place that would model family life in daily living; a place that would allow for "farmers" to learn work skills, help produce marketable crops and give opportunities for positive community service.

"We felt like it was a calling, something we were supposed to do," said Joe.

So on a cold, winter day in 1983, Joe and June looked at a plot of land on Glass Pike in Scott County that was for sale. "The only thing there was one house and a barn," said Joe, "and looking back, we wonder what we saw there."

But there was something special about the location, the Richeys sensed, so the two prayerfully decided to pursue buying the property—at a cost of $128,000. It would be an uphill battle to make it happen.

Specifically, the two would have to sell an unusual idea to a bank in order to get financing.

"The first bank we talked to nearly threw us out," recalled Joe, "but the next one offered to lend us the money if we could get them a $51,000 down payment."

Not capable of self-financing the Quest Farm property, a great amount of serious fund-raising was essential. "We sent out a letter to possible contributors on the Friday after Thanksgiving," said June, "and we were surprised by the response. It was better than we expected."

The funds came in but were about $20,000 short. That's when what Joe called a "miracle" occurred.

"With only two weeks before our deadline for getting the down payment together, we received a check in the mail from a gentleman from Oklahoma for that amount," said Joe. The property deal closed, and Joe and June now needed residents and a program.

More obstacles appeared as Quest Farm opened. "A neighbor blasted us in the local newspaper," explained Joe. "The lady tried to stop what she called 'undesirables' from living on Glass Pike. She even convinced some other neighbors to sign a petition against us."

The Richeys, disappointed but not devastated, continued to take steps forward. "We moved in as quietly as we could, with no fanfare," said Joe.

Soon, another challenge presented itself, one that now seems humorous.

"We knew nothing about raising tobacco (a crop Quest Farm no longer raises) or other farming," Joe said with a laugh, "and one day, the husband of the neighbor who had given us so much trouble came over as we were trying to get the ground ready for tobacco planting." The neighbor asked Joe about what he was doing. Joe tried to explain, but was not convincing. The neighbor offered to get his tractor.

"The neighbor went back to his place, drove his tractor and plow over and showed us how to do it. The lady later died, but we became good friends of them and they've helped us a lot," Joe said.

As the Richeys and the resident farmers gained experience in their agrarian-business lifestyle, and by hiring competent farm managers along the way, they attracted a solid local market for their produce—items such as asparagus, cabbage, peppers and chrysanthemums.

Quest's farmers played important roles in the start-up and present success. "Our farmers have many different ability levels," said Joe. "One person drives a tractor. There are four or five who can handle riding lawn mowers. The women work in our greenhouses and with our asparagus and flowers."

The work hours generally run from 9:30 to 4:00. A mentoring process goes on among the farmers. "We let those with more ability help those with less ability," continued Joe. "We talk a lot about safety, and we've been blessed beyond words that we've not had a serious accident."

Joe and June spoke glowingly of some individual resident farmers.

"Keith has an uncanny ability to handle farm machinery," he said, "and he has learned to take responsibility." Buddy, in his mid-seventies, "has learned to enjoy life. For a long time, Buddy wanted to work all the time and didn't want to take time to play at all," Joe explained. The Richeys also raved about Bob, a resident who does wonderful crocheting and even sells it for extra spending money. "He learned when he was a kid, and he does it left-handed," said June. Then there is the lady who speaks very little, but "who knows where everything is," said Joe. "If you need to find something, she's the one to ask."

Not only do the farmers do meaningful and productive work at the Glass Pike address, they also are involved in community-help projects. "Joel, our program director, has them working with Habitat houses. They also help deliver meals with the Meals on Wheels program," said Joe.

A balanced program is emphasized, with Friday afternoons devoted to banking activities in Georgetown. "We encourage them not to spend everything they earn from what we pay them," said Joe, "so that they will have money when we do vacations."

Trips to the local bowling alley and Wal-Mart are also frequent rituals, along with periodic parties on the premises. Often, residents take solo walks on the property, and a few like to drive a golf cart for fun. "We offer lots of freedom here," said Joe.

There are three brick, comfortable houses for Quest Farm residents, with six living in each building. Two houses contain men, the other women. All include house managers who help as needed.

Quest Farm has plans for an activity shelter to be built. The facilities will provide an enhanced place to have educational programs and activities that outside community members volunteer to present to the residents. Church youth groups of 20-30 often come to Quest for short-time projects. "Those kids really work, too," said June.

The Richeys give much credit for the community support to David Waters, Quest's former executive director, program director Joel Laumas, along with Mike Krieg, operations manager and all the house managers. "June and I are getting to the place where we don't have the energy to be as involved, but we feel that with the staff we have here, we're in good shape."

Waters is impressed with the work of Joe and June. "When I came here, I just sat back in my chair and said 'Wow!' They were part of an insane adventure without any training," noted Waters. "They had just a dream and a calling."

Besides the staff at Quest Farm, the Richeys are grateful for another couple who were there from the beginning in offering encouragement and financial support for the project.

"Don and Dora Putnam helped us a lot, and we owe them a debt of gratitude," said Joe. "They have always been involved in causes, including a home for 'wayward girls' before they worked with us."

Joe Richey spoke of more dreams involving Quest Farm. "Someday we'd like to build a retirement home for our residents here on the land. It would be a place for them to relax. They can sit on the front porch and rock, or whatever. I'd also like to write a book about Quest Farm and explain how it all came to be."

Joe and June Richey have simply done what they felt their God wanted them to do. They've always wanted to help others gain an opportunity to follow their own dreams.

To that end, look no further than that special place out on Glass Pike, where two compassionate people steadfastly followed a lofty quest to serve.

Judy Sizemore

'Circuit Rider' of Arts Helps Improve Lives, Communities

If wholeheartedly extending oneself to communicate the benefits of the arts can be likened to the religious practice of spreading the gospel, Judy Sizemore is truly an arts evangelist. She's akin to the Methodist circuit riders of old, traveling the winding roads, searching for listening ears, seeking open hearts, and hoping to influence joyful conversions. Some might say that she is "called."

Her canon is formed from the fruits of her own personal experience, that of an accomplished writer and poet, along with the changed lives she's observed. Her message is simple—the arts are a bridge to the very soul of every person, and the same brings out the very best in each.

Most significantly, Judy Sizemore, in her loving, patient way, inspires others to a special kind of personal awareness and redemption.

Just ask friends and colleagues, such as Susan Mitchell. "When people talk to her and about her it is with great respect because she knows art, she knows artists, she knows that people in general are artists at their core," she said. "Her ideas are grand, they are full of life and they are possible. She makes you want to work with her because you know that whatever she touches will be a success on a much bigger scale than you could have imagined on your own."

Judy Sizemore

Sometimes in a freelance way, at other times as a contract worker with the Kentucky Arts Council, Sizemore travels to all parts of the state, meeting people where they are, both geographically and figuratively.

Observe the ways she works since she began her work in 1988. Maybe it's teaching a creative-writing activity to a group of rural third-graders, some of them with dyslexia. Or guiding their parents to become effective volunteer tutors to their children's classmates.

In speaking passionately of those with dyslexia, Sizemore sees great potential despite the reading difficulties they face. She believes in teaching to their strengths. "Children with dyslexia are extraordinarily creative," the Jackson County resident said. "Many of them are very talented at drawing and painting and visual arts."

A strong understanding of the role of multiple intelligences has also guided her instruction.

"Rather than just giving kids continual remedial work, we should help them use their strengths to learn what is difficult for them," Sizemore said. "You just have to meet people where they are. I want every child to have art in the classroom, and we need to use ways of teaching that use something they know about from their own experiences."

To the New Hampshire-born dynamo, her teaching goal, eventually, is always self-actualization, which then brings a larger and positive social change in communities.

Sizemore may be observed working with a beaten-down, but flickeringly hopeful, group of drug-court participants, resourcefully pulling in an assortment of musicians, visual artists, or dramatic performers bent on sharing their passions and making a difference with their audience.

You might see Sizemore involved in a planning session with a county extension agent in eastern Kentucky, hoping to exhort community members to record their own unique oral history—then to archive the results in the local public library, available for future generations to appreciate.

She writes and advocates for feminist or environmental causes, often published widely outside the state. Eloquently, Sizemore appeals to the best instincts in her audience to plead the case of social justice.

Sizemore's imprint on the arts culture can be seen even to casual observers around the state. In rural areas all around Kentucky, there's artwork appearing on the sides of barns—in the form of beautifully crafted quilt paintings, part of the "Quilt Trails" project. Yes, Judy Sizemore is involved in helping with that endeavor, too.

She worked with country music singer Ricky Skaggs to produce "More than Music: A Heritage Driving Tour of Kentucky's Route 23." The project involved bringing together artists, private organizations and state bureaus to create a self-guided driving trip. Sizemore wrote the script, which involved interviewing residents along the eastern corridor. She envisions the tour guide helping economically and increasing the cultural pride of the area.

"She clearly understands the power of the arts to change attitudes," said Sue Massek, director of The Kentucky Foundation for Women, from which Sizemore won the coveted 2005 Sallie Bingham Award for service in support of feminist causes. "She continually honors the gifts of women to their families, communities, cultures and the world ... [and] is one of Kentucky's top experts at using art to create and build community."

Gwenda Adkins has partnered with Sizemore in several community-based projects, including one called "Arts and Healing." Adkins marvels at the way her friend has courageously handled breast cancer and continues to share her arts message.

"One of the strongest women I know. She's a fighter and winner," said Adkins.

Sizemore addresses her personal cancer fight and showcases her environmental sensitivities with her collection of poems, *Asymmetry* (Motes, 2007), offering smooth, reassuring words and colorful images.

Susan Mitchell calls her "a brilliant writer," and Octavia Sexton, a colleague partnering with Sizemore on a recent oral history project, spoke of Sizemore's "talent of using words to form an exquisite expression of herself. She is able to release a part of her soul and share it with others in a message of 250 words or less."

Overall, Sizemore has over 300 published writing pieces credited and has continuously used her talents as a writer-in-residence in state-wide programs. Ironically, her early plunge into magazine writing consisted of a host of articles written for boating magazines—a natural outgrowth of her love of the outdoors, and at a time "when my husband and I lived in Florida—and [where] we ate a lot of the local shrimp," she said with a grin.

By all accounts, Judy Sizemore embraces life to the fullest. She is positive; she is passionate. She's proud of her daughter, adopted at three days old and who possesses her mother's zest for living—and is now a college graduate and mother of two. Additionally, Sizemore has enjoyed a long and good marriage to her husband Dennis, who's art of choices are photography and sculpting.

She has a legion of friends who love her because she has loved them.

Truly, Judy Sizemore's enthusiasm for arts and her love for people who are hurting helps create exciting networks and better lives. She leaves tools of fulfillment that will continue to grow fruit and bring hope, even after this circuit rider moves along to the next gathering who await her compelling message.

Joan Smith

Pro-life Advocate Uses Maternity Home
to Save Children and Teach Mothers

There was a time in America's past when unmarried, pregnant young ladies would "go away," have their babies in a hospital and leave out the back door in order not to be seen. An adoption agency would systematically process the newborn to a waiting party, then receive payment for services. For those involved personally and for those presumed "guilty," the matter was one not to be discussed, mainly because of the humiliating stigma attached.

"The whole thing was considered a very shameful experience, and it was as if they made it as hard on the mother as they could," noted Joan Smith, who has devoted her adult life to helping young, unwed mothers navigate this tumultuous time.

Smith, as an emergency-room and labor-delivery nurse before she gave birth to her own two boys in the early '70s, saw her passion for human life and dignity develop roots. Along with her own physical complications that resulted in a miscarriage, the experiences motivated her to make it a nearly full-time avocation. "When I saw the first baby born, I knew that's where I wanted to be," said Smith.

Judging by her productive pro-life work—and success over many years—her instincts seem totally correct.

Joan Smith

Smith left the nursing profession about the time that the Supreme Court ruled on the legality of abortion, but she did not leave the nurturing of young life. She spoke and participated frequently in groups and gatherings, passionately advocating pro-life issues. She was involved in PLUS Line, an organization for distressed young women with unplanned pregnancies to call for emergency guidance—started by both doctors and nurses, who, according to Smith, "were the ones who really started the pro-life movement."

In 1989, she founded St. Elizabeth's Regional Maternity Center, a Catholic Charities agency, in New Albany, Ind. Some philosophical differences with St. Elizabeth's led Smith in 1997 to start a new work in nearby Jeffersonville called Noah's Ark Children's Village. The mission of the Noah's Ark program was to provide a loving environment for abused or neglected foster children in a community-oriented setting.

In 2006, Smith, a New Albany, Indiana, native now living in Jeffersonville, took a look around the city of Louisville, where she attends church and has many friends. She explained that "there had been five maternity homes … and they had all closed their doors." That fact set her focus on the unmet needs of this population in the city.

"When the last one closed, I said 'I'm going to start a maternity home [in Louisville],'" remarked Smith.

The Lifehouse Center is now thriving at 2710 Riedling Drive in Louisville. Smith is the director of the maternity home, a place of hope "for pregnant young women who have made the courageous choice to have their babies and need our support." There are currently spaces for eight residents. The program is Christian-based, but inter-denominational.

House mothers live with the residents to offer guidance and support. For those who choose to place their baby for adoption, help is given in the process. Lifehouse takes no fee for the adoption, however.

"That might tend to influence the way we counsel the person," Smith said. "It is important to know that by not charging for an adoption the mother can never say that we cared more for the baby than we did for her."

No government money is used, and the non-profit maternity home deals with a cost of about $800 per day to operate. The money comes from gifts from private individuals, businesses and foundations.

Smith involves herself in Lifehouse work about sixty hours per week. "I fly by the seat of my pants a lot, but my training as an ER nurse has helped," she said. "I believe with all my heart that God will provide."

She speaks at churches, clubs and sometimes on radio shows. She has a reputation as open and transparent, both in regard to talking about admission for interested persons and to the public about the home's program.

But she also is known as being diplomatic. When the news broke that Lifehouse would become a part of the neighborhood, some nervous concern surfaced. "Within two hours, I met in someone's living room with the [neighborhood] association's members and they became very supportive, even offering to help," said Smith.

The rules for staying at Lifehouse are strict, Smith admits, and some people are not suited for the high expectations. She's even had to dismiss residents who didn't cooperate.

"It hurts," she said, "when you see the potential in some young women, and then to see them turn their back on what they can become as a mother."

Dr. Dennis Kaufman, a part-time licensed pastoral counselor at Lifehouse who, along with Smith, founded the Center, praised Smith as both "visionary and energetic ... a person who's passion in these matters runs deep."

Smith's focus to help has found company with multitudes of others who support Lifehouse. She talked about people like Val Henson, a building contractor who has donated much of the work on the Riedling Drive house—"a house," said Smith, "we had no money for when we bought." There are more stories like a young man who mowed the lawn because he just wanted to help; an accountant keeps the books without pay; a woman who made the house's curtains; and local chefs have provided meals for residents.

"My goal is to present the mission and hope that people want to be a part of it. Lifehouse is not me, or anything I did," Smith said. "I'm just an instrument."

Becky Edmonson, a friend, remarked, "She gets others excited about Lifehouse and they want to follow. What drives Joan is she has a calling from God. Her courage and strength comes from the Lord. The sacrifice is [that] the work never ends. You can only do what she has done if you have a supportive husband, and she does. I admire Joan because the work is hard and you can suffer from burnout, but she has built three homes, three separate ministries."

Winnie Walker volunteers at Lifehouse, as well as formerly at Noah's Ark. She knows Joan Smith well. "Joan is not just about 'saving the children,'" said Walker. "She has a love for the family surrounding them. She has a willingness to sacrifice her pleasures and desires. She could be sitting home and playing golf, bridge or shopping. She lives her faith."

Ron Nabors

Corporate Executive Makes World Impact

Ron Nabors has wrestled with few major personal failures in his life.

He was raised modestly in Versailles, but he was well-fed and enjoyed the blessings of a loving family. Turned down by his girlfriend the first time he proposed marriage, she later accepted and the couple have enjoyed a long and happy life together. He came up one semester short of graduating from Georgetown College, but that fact didn't interfere with smashing success over many years as an executive in the corporate business world.

A good and prosperous man, Nabors still lacked something, and it gnawed at him. When he started his duties as chief executive officer of Christian Blind Mission-United States (CBM–US) a few years back, he gained what he didn't yet have—world impact that really mattered.

For Nabors, and many others, it's made all the difference.

CBM is an international organization of compassion that seeks to better the lives of those with disabilities who live in the poorest countries of the world, a population that numbers over 500 million. CBM works with the disabilities of blindness, deafness, physical, and mental disabilities. The organization is doing its part to improve the challenging situation.

Ron Nabors

"Last year, CBM touched, in some form or fashion, over eighteen million people," noted Nabors. Quite a profound accomplishment.

The preparation for such an enormous, positive endeavor for Nabors—one that might properly be called a "daring rescue"— likely began as a youngster after hearing about his father's heroic act at an electric-power plant in Woodford County.

"There was an explosion at the plant," said Nabors of the Kentucky Utilities location at Tyrone, "and people told me how he crawled across the floor in a smoke-filled room and knew just what valves to turn off, saving the plant from blowing up. The courage and character of my father impacted my life greatly."

Nabors remembered, too, the bonding influence of father-son time camping together along the banks of the Kentucky River.

Besides the love and admiration he felt for his family, the folks at Versailles Baptist Church, where Nabors was actively involved, supported him in a big way. Nabors appreciated them but the mutual admiration eventually proved somewhat worrisome.

"I believe I was heavily influenced by the church members to enter the pastoral ministry," he said. "It was just something that was expected."

And Nabors met those expectations, starting in a small way at first. He graduated from Woodford County High School and enrolled at nearby Georgetown College, majoring in philosophy and religion. He was dating future wife, Linda, when he received an opportunity to minister part-time with a tiny, rural church in Franklin County.

"They had a white clap-board building with a pot-bellied stove and an old pump organ on a dead-end road," he said, "and they needed a preacher."

Nabors grinned when he explained the circumstances: "The church wrote a letter to the college requesting someone, and they said that he didn't even have to be good." He took the job for a less-than-princely sum of $5 per Sunday. He and Linda were well received. It was an early indicator of his ability to lead.

"The people at that church just needed someone to hold their hand," he said of the congregation of about thirty.

Now with experience in church ministry, though young and still in school, he accepted another church position at Plainview Baptist Church, near Maysville, in 1968. The membership was larger and there were greater responsibilities.

"I was there when lots of children came into the world and we had baptismal services in the creek," said Nabors. "It was a wonderful ministry."

In June 1968, Ron and Linda married not long after he "got down on my knees and asked Linda in front of Giddings Hall on the Georgetown campus." It proved to be a smart move.

Another church ministry followed, this time in Lexington. But with family responsibilities increasing with the birth of a son, he left school and took another job as a hearing-aids salesman in the mountains of Kentucky. Nabors performed well and comfortably in that role. Additionally, he considered the business another form of ministry, a way to improve others' lives.

It was an idea that stuck close to his heart.

When he received another offer to take a larger pastoral ministry position near Paris, he accepted, but fought off feelings of restlessness he invariably experienced at all of his church stops along the way. Church members generally were happy with the work of Nabors, but he had doubts about whether he was truly "called" to the pastoral ministry.

So after a few years at Spears Mill Baptist, where he had a local radio program, a newspaper column, and a hospital and jail ministry, Nabors decided to leave and become a salesperson for the Pitney-Bowes Company.

"The most painful decision I ever made was leaving the pastoral ministry," he said. He understood the reason he left, though. "The voice I had followed [previously] into the pastoral ministry were those wonderful people of the Versailles Baptist Church."

By now, Nabors and his wife had increased their family to three children, so the incentive to increase their income was strong. He did, by traveling throughout eastern Kentucky and selling the company's office projects. He made $350 per month plus a very good commission. He worked hard and saved more by staying in

$9.95 hotels. Though now in sales, Nabors continued to focus on a "ministry" frame of mind in his new vocation.

He had a strong sales mantra that guided him.

"My objective was to help customers improve their businesses rather than to sell them something," said Nabors. "There's a difference."

Soon, Nabors won a "Salesman of the Year" award from the company, especially notable because there were 3,000 competing for the award. His sense of restlessness had disappeared, and still, he felt like he was being faithful to his religious commitment to help others first.

The upper management of Pitney-Bowes was impressed, and the young man from Versailles accepted an offer of promotion, one which would move the Nabors family northward to Youngstown, Ohio. The position there was a huge challenge.

"I showed up at Youngstown, and it was closed," he said. By that, he meant that Youngstown was in the midst of a severe recession. Businesses were closing and people weren't buying.

"There was all kinds of negativity at our offices. I had to tell our employees that there was a way out of this and not to give up," Nabors said.

He retrained the staff, incorporating "people ministry" ideas that had worked for him in eastern Kentucky. The Youngstown location of Pitney-Bowes became the company's second-leading district office.

Nabors was promoted to the company's headquarters in Connecticut, where again his leadership helped the Pitney-Bowes bottom line grow. Then, off to Baton Rouge, Louisana, where a turnaround was badly needed.

"The Baton Rouge office was performing just awful. Interestingly. everybody there was male, so I started interviewing women," he said. "We started winning sales awards, most of them by women, and we were named the number one branch for Pitney-Bowes. We started at number 99 out of 99."

Nabors also became an advocate for women in the workplace, appearing on television, radio and doing speaking engagements. At that time, according to Nabors, "most major corporations in the industry were almost all male."

And then came Omaha, then Chicago and after that, New York, where he led a major turnaround of Pitney-Bowes's largest office.

When the company moved his family to Australia, where his time there was "marginally successful," a new and exhilarating experience powerfully touched his heart.

"We had a subsidiary sales and service company in Papua New Guinea, where we helped support a school for indigenous people," Nabors said. "Through this school, we were able to take people out of poverty, provide education and training, and employ them in our company."

This effort led to dramatically reducing the expatriates in Papua and replacing them with people, he said, "who needed and deserved the opportunity." Nabors was recognized by the Papua prime minister for his efforts to nationalize the workforce.

"This was about business but also a major effort to bring equity, inclusion and pride to local people living in poverty," said Nabors. "It was very fulfilling."

There were other stops along the career path, including ten years as a senior executive with Bell & Howell and a couple of software companies. He had by now made his mark as a high achiever. But with all those years of experience in the business and corporate world, Nabors decided to take a break to do some introspection, to think about his future hopes and dreams. He sought to answer the questions: "Is there some way I can take my corporate skills and use them for something other than helping another corporation's bottom line? What will be my legacy?"

Nabors was interested in doing a work that had even more long-term benefits than he had already influenced.

Which brings us to Christian Blind Mission, where Nabors now uses his expertise to improve the lives of vulnerable persons around the globe. He has been CEO of CBM-US since 2007, and he loves to talk about the international ministry of the organization.

"Every minute, a child is born blind in the developing world and fifty percent of them die within two years. One of the leading cause of preventable blindness in the developing world is vitamin A deficiency," said Nabors. "We distribute hundreds of thousands of vitamin A tablets every year."

Nabors praised an "incredible furniture-maker," named Boniface, who CBM had mentored and taught skills to help him be productive in the aftermath of blindness caused by measles. He told how in developing regions of the world clubfoot is a problem, a condition "which often allows one only to crawl, with no chance of getting an education or having a normal life. They are often beggars." Through CBM's medical staff working with these persons, however, "clubfoot is completely repairable, and it allows them to go to school, be productive, find a mate and have quality of life."

Part of the CBM mission is to make micro-loans to people who are poor and with disabilities to help start small businesses.

"The loan must be repaid," said Nabors. "We want to teach the recipients *how to fish rather than to just receive a fish.*"

The organization's hope is that the needed assistance economically and educationally, given by the staff will, said Nabors, "eventually allow us to walk away" from such intense care for the previously vulnerable as they begin to stand independently.

Nabors talks ruefully of the shame the disabled poor feel who "many times are considered 'cursed.' They're marginalized," he said. He knows that simple medical procedures can often powerfully change their lives for the better.

In his position, Nabors travels widely, seeking funds to attack these challenges, to advocate passionately for this population, and to live his personal religious faith "by honoring my commitment to the Kingdom [of God]."

Eric Fruge, a friend who has observed Nabors' servant-leadership style, said: "Ron's strength is that he always has a passion for the success of those who work under him, and he yearns to see others experience fulfillment in their lives."

Nabors has always been that way, but now he is making that impact on the entire world.

For more information about CBM,
visit http://cbmus.org

Jerry Hayes

A Passion for Restoring Cabins and Family Values

Jerry Hayes remembers vividly a special two-week period in his childhood at age five, a time he spent with his grandparents on Mauldlin Branch Road in Jackson County.

"Pa" and "Granny" Clark showed him family, nature and religious faith. The couple showed him how to exist in rustic living quarters, how to raise food for the family, and how to have good, clean fun—inexpensively.

Jerry Hayes saw on Mauldlin Branch that there were kindnesses given, kindnesses received. He embraced all of it, and when he grew to adulthood, he decided to do something about it.

That experience in August 1951 ignited a passion in Hayes to recreate that memorable feeling, that strong sense of place and individual epiphany he enjoyed in those several days almost six decades ago. And today, after fourteen years of concentrated, patient and sometimes frustrating effort, he has come pretty close to doing just that by creating the Brush Arbor Appalachian Pioneer Homestead, a twenty-five-acre plot of land in Renfro Valley, in Rockcastle County, that includes twelve beautifully restored log cabins salvaged from five different states. Hayes has financed the project almost entirely from his own resources.

People come from far places to visit, as the lure of Brush Arbor and its nostalgic, peaceful ambience attracts thousands annually, with "sixteen countries represented," said Hayes.

Hayes, an eighth-generation Irish descendent of Patrick and Amelia Hayes, who entered Kentucky through the Cumberland Gap, recalled the special time that started the whole venture for the young city boy residing in Hamilton County, Ohio.

Jerry Hayes

"I kept after my mom and dad to let me stay two weeks with my grandparents. When I got there, I sat there on the creek bank for ten minutes—crying," he remembered. "It was the first time I had been away from home. But those two weeks were the most incredible time of my life. I learned to appreciate things. I learned what love was."

Love and a sense of responsibility to something bigger than himself drives Hayes today.

While sitting on the front porch of the log building serving as a store, exhibit center and main office for Brush Arbor, the devoutly religious and emotional Hayes showed wet eyes and struggled with words as he talked about the on-going project, started in 1996, when he was forty-nine. "I bought a John Deere tractor to use to clean up the property. I picked up rocks, cleared brush and didn't know anything about what I was doing," he said.

The first rescued cabin to land at Brush Arbor came from a location about three miles from where Pa and Granny Clark lived. It was an 1860 structure belonging to James and Lisa Pennington, and, like all the other eleven cabins, is authentically restored with the original logs in place. The buildings are nestled in an open meadow of lush grass bordered by native trees, a peaceful sanctuary set off a comfortable distance from the road. Over in Lincoln County, there are seven other buildings in storage, with "one belonging to Daniel Boone's daughter," Hayes said.

There has been some significant publicity about Brush Arbor. An Associated Press story about the unique venture was printed all over the United States. Movie scenes from "The Stephen Foster Story" were shot there. Country music entertainer Tom T. Hall produced a special video at Brush Arbor, and Kentucky Educational TV aired a special story.

But Hayes would like to see an expansion of what Brush Arbor can offer in order to touch more lives in a significant way.

"I see us having two walking trails here, and a natural amphitheatre. I'd like us to have a restaurant serving Appalachian-style food. I'd like to see pastors, missionaries, and kids come to this place ... a retreat where people can tell stories and learn about their traditions and culture."

Dr. Dora Bronston, a friend of Hayes and a college teacher from Middletown, Ohio, has watched the growth of Brush Arbor with admiring eyes. "His efforts have made it possible for people to reach out and touch history rather than merely read about it in history books," she said.

Brush Arbor costs about $20,000 a year to keep up, said Hayes. That is not an easy responsibility for him to handle, as he has had his share of personal financial challenges in recent years.

Bronston remarked that "with absolutely no public funding, zero tax dollars, no local, state, or federal funding, Jerry Hayes has provided every single dollar to make this possible, with the exception of a retired minister from Frankfort who assisted in the funding of the old log church."

For Jerry Hayes, the only thing better than Brush Arbor would be to go back for a few weeks in time to his grandparents' home on Mauldlin Branch. For now, he just hopes to capture a bit of it for others to enjoy.

Restoring cabins, and souls, you might say.

For those interested in learning more about Brush Arbor,
go to website http://Brush-Arbor.com

Dr. Andrew Moore

Physician's 'Surgery on Sunday' Helps Many

Young Andy Moore watched his father, who happened to be the first plastic surgeon in Lexington, perform genuine acts of compassion to financially strapped patients on a regular basis.

"He would sometimes accept a chicken, or apples—or anything of value they had as pay for their services. As far as I know, he never turned down anyone who couldn't pay," said Moore. "My father led by example. He mentored me."

Andy didn't take to the lesson of personal responsibility immediately, however. He flunked out of the University of Kentucky as an undergraduate. He did so poorly that he was told by the school "not to bother coming back."

Fortunately, an act of mercy allowed him to be accepted at Transylvania University, under the watchful eye of a mentor, he recovered and succeeded magnificently. Later, he was accepted into the UK Medical School program, then transitioned into Vanderbilt where he trained as a plastic surgeon.

Today, Dr. Andrew Moore, like his now-deceased father, practices as a plastic surgeon in Lexington. He's never been offered a chicken or apples to pay for his medical services, but he is like-minded in offering caring assistance to those working people who are unable to afford basic outpatient surgery because they have no health insurance.

Dr. Andrew Moore

Since 2005, Dr. Moore has led a team of upwards of 700 volunteers—surgeons, physicians, nurses, medical assistants, church workers and anyone else desiring to offer their time and love to Surgery on Sunday (SOS). It is a program that administers free outpatient surgery, one Sunday morning per month, to a great number of appreciative, deserving individuals who otherwise would not receive the services. So far more than 3,000 surgeries, involving 110 types of procedures, have been performed by SOS.

On a recent Sunday in November at the Lexington Surgery Center, May Newton waited for her husband, Glen Samual Newton, to return from the operating room. He had double-hernia surgery, a procedure Newton had simply postponed because of financial issues.

The two had married only the day before, but the opportunity for care at SOS came, and the Newtons responded. "It's a blessing for my husband," said May. "So many people fall through the cracks and can't get insurance."

Because of the program, Glen Newton will now be able to go back to work and be a thoroughly productive member of his community.

One family waited as their six-year-old daughter had a "piece of corn" removed from her ear. The father, who called himself a "granite worker," heard about SOS from their church. Across the room, Deandre Greenup waited for her boyfriend to have a troublesome screw removed from his knee that had been put there during another procedure. The pain had bothered him at his workplace and interfered with his work.

None of the people in the room complained of the wait time or of any inconvenience. They were glad for the opportunity to be there, and all had a sense of appreciation showing on their faces. In a country where reportedly over forty million do not have health insurance, the patients in Dr. Moore's SOS program were being served anyway, with no cost for the services but likely a good investment for society.

Moore is blessed with volunteer surgeons like Dr. Bill Bowles, who regularly practices in the Breathitt County town of Jackson. Bowles makes two trips per month to Lexington for the SOS program, one to do surgeries and another to do pre-ops and post-ops. "My way of giving back to the community," he says. "The people who we work with in SOS are so appreciative of us because they know it is volunteer help."

Bowles marvels at Dr. Moore's influence in starting SOS. "This is a program that can't be run by the seat of the pants," said Bowles. "It needs to be legal and safe. Dr. Moore has been very persistent in getting the program going."

The idea of an SOS-type of program started in Moore's mind back in the mid-1990s. "When insurance companies got more involved with fees," said Moore, "things always got discounted. Then those who had no insurance, who needed to self pay, had to pay *more* than anyone else for the same medical care."

Many people simply avoided important care because of costs. Obviously, a program like Moore envisioned was compelling, but there were roadblocks. It took a while to happen.

While sitting in one of his many meetings in about 2003, Dr. Moore tossed out his idea for discussion to those sitting around the table. "I think I can get volunteers and I believe I have a place to have the program, but we need money and I need help in handling the legal part of doing it," he recalled.

On this day, he was lucky. Almost providentially, there happened to be a grant writer in the gathering. "She told me she could get me the money, and she did—$235,000. I knew then that I was locked in to doing this thing," said Moore.

"I was president of the Lexington Surgery Center at the time," said Moore, "and so they agreed to give us their facility on one Sunday a month and let us use their supplies. We got a pretty good basis of people together, and we had to get malpractice insurance." A lawyer agreed to offer his services to work out the legalities. The working group hired a person to run the program and in 2005, SOS began operating.

Moore likes the happy buzz that surrounds volunteers and patients alike on SOS days.

"If I can get you there one time, I've got you hooked," said Moore. "That's what I tell everyone when I speak about the program. The volunteers are always saying 'Can I help you?' and looking for something to do."

Some come from out of town locations like Murray or Louisville. There are churches that supply meals, and social workers and language interpreters give of their time and skills.. "They've just come together by pure luck or by divine providence...or whatever," said Moore.

Moore wants to see much done because of the great need he sees. "We're about a year and a half behind on gall bladder surgeries," he said. "We want to consider doing SOS on two Sundays a month, and I've talked to people all over the country who are interested in starting similar programs."

Moore likely will win others to a program like SOS. He has an amiable personality, always looking at the bright side.

Just ask Mary Ellen Amato, who worked with Moore's father and knew the young, often mischievous Andy. She remembered visiting him when he attended St. Joseph Prep School, in Bardstown, when he was a teenager.

"We would come to see him and they had him on the garbage detail. He was always getting demerits. But, he always had a smile on his face."

Moore's mother, Peggy, another volunteer at SOS, added, "Andy was always into things, always happy-go-lucky."

Volunteer nurse Patti Fowler said that Moore "has always made patients feel at ease, always has a joke to share, and is always relaxed."

It's often said that great things can be accomplished if one does not care who gets the credit.

According to Dr. Andrew Moore, much of the credit for Surgery on Sunday can go to his father, who modeled true servanthood.

To learn more about Surgery on Sunday,
visit http://surgeryonsunday.org

Photography credits

Charles Whitaker (Kym Hitchcock)
Kevin Gunderson (Gunderson's personal collection)
Robin Schmidt (CurtisGPhotography.com, Chandler, AZ)
Ron Kibbey (Sabrina Puckett)
Charles and Elaine Fuerniss (Madonna Courtney)
Evelyn Johnson Seals (Seals's personal collection)
Dale Faughn (Faughn's personal collection)
Mary Lou Boal (Boal's personal collection)
Chester and Ann Grundy (Holifield Photography, Lexington, KY)
Judy Hensley (Rhonda Robinson)
Brian Huybers (Michele Huybers)
Roy Pullam (Pullam's personal collection)
Sandy and Jerry Tucker (Galilean Home Ministries, Inc.)
Dr. George Wright (Prairie View University Public Relations)
Shirley Donathan (thestudiophotography.com, Mt. Sterling, KY)
Bill Gordon (Suzi Marques)
Fanestia Massey (Massey's personal collection)
Joe and June Richey (Richeys' personal collection)
Judy Sizemore (Dennis Sizemore)
Ron Nabors (Courtesy of CMDA)
Jerry Hayes (Greerphotography.com, Lexington, KY)
Dr. Andrew Moore (Surgery on Sunday, Inc.)